STUDIES IN ECONOMIC AND SO

This series, specially commissioned ~~~~~~~~~~ History
Society, provides a guide to the current interpretations of the key
themes of economic and social history in which advances have
recently been made or in which there has been significant debate.

Originally entitled 'Studies in Economic History', in 1974 the
series had its scope extended to include topics in social history, and
the new series title, 'Studies in Economic and Social History',
signalises this development.

The series gives readers access to the best work done, helps them
to draw their own conclusions in major fields of study, and by
means of the critical bibliography in each book guides them in the
selection of further reading. The aim is to provide a springboard to
further work rather than a set of pre-packaged conclusions or
short-cuts.

ECONOMIC HISTORY SOCIETY

The Economic History Society, which numbers over 3000 members, publishes the *Economic History Review* four times a year (free
to members) and holds an annual conference. Enquiries about
membership should be addressed to the Assistant Secretary, Economic History Society, Peterhouse, Cambridge. Full-time students
may join at special rates.

STUDIES IN ECONOMIC AND SOCIAL HISTORY

Edited for the Economic History Society by L. A. Clarkson

PUBLISHED

OTHER TITLES ARE IN PREPARATION

Proto-Industrialization: The First Phase of Industrialization?

*Prepared for
the Economic History Society by*

L. A. CLARKSON
Queen's University, Belfast

MACMILLAN

First published 1985

Published by
Higher and Further Education Division
MACMILLAN PUBLISHERS LTD
Houndmills, Basingstoke, Hampshire RG21 2XS
and London
Companies and Representatives
throughout the world

Printed in Hong Kong

British Library Cataloguing in Publication Data
Clarkson, L.A.
Proto-industrialization: the first phase of
industrialization?—(Studies in economic and social history)
1. Europe—Industries—History
I. Title   II. Economic History Society
III. Series
338.094   HC240
ISBN 0–333–34392–1

Contents

Acknowledgements

This book was accepted by the Economic History Society when Professer Smout was editor of the series but was finished after I had taken over. Accordingly, I have turned to others to scrutinize my text. I am grateful to Dr. R. B. Outhwaite for sceptical comments characteristic of Cambridge; to my colleague, Dr. K. D. Brown, for exercising skills sharpened by his editorial duties with another series; and to another colleague, Mr J. McAllister, whose perception of what students will tolerate is matched only by his unrivalled knowledge of the early-modern period. I have accepted some of their advice; the faults remaining are my own. I wish to thank, also, Sr Anne McKernan, O.P. of the University of Michigan for discussing with me her researches on the linen industry in County Armagh.

Note on References

References in the text within square brackets relate to the numbered items in the Bibliography, followed, where necessary, by the page numbers in italics, for example [1,7–9].

Editor's Preface

WHEN this series was established in 1968 the first editor, the late Professor M. W. Flinn, laid down three guiding principles. The books should be concerned with important fields of economic history; they should be surveys of the current state of scholarship rather than a vehicle for the specialist views of the authors, and above all, they were to be introductions to their subject and not 'a set of pre-packaged conclusions'. These aims were admirably fulfilled by Professor Flinn and by his successor, Professor T. C. Smout, who took over the series in 1977. As it passes to its third editor and approaches its third decade, the principles remain the same.

Nevertheless, times change, even though principles do not. The series was launched when the study of economic history was burgeoning and new findings and fresh interpretations were threatening to overwhelm students – and sometimes their teachers. The series has expanded its scope, particularly in the area of social history – although the distinction between 'economic' and 'social' is sometimes hard to recognize and even more difficult to sustain. It has also extended geographically; its roots remain firmly British, but an increasing number of titles is concerned with the economic and social history of the wider world. However, some of the early titles can no longer claim to be introductions to the current state of scholarship; and the discipline as a whole lacks the heady growth of the 1960s and early 1970s. To overcome the first problem a number of new editions, or entirely new works, have been commissioned – some have already appeared. To deal with the second, the aim remains to publish up-to-date introductions to important areas of debate. If the series can demonstrate to students and their teachers the importance of the discipline of economic and social history and excite its further study, it will continue the task so ably begun by its first two editors.

The Queen's University of Belfast   L. A. CLARKSON
                                                      General Editor

1 *'Proto-industrialization':*
The urge to generalize

In the early 1970s an ugly new word – 'proto-industrialization' – entered the literature of economic history and since then has rapidly colonized books, articles and even undergraduate essays, spawning additional abstractions as it goes along. A new historical generalization had arrived, chiefly through the efforts of Franklin Mendels [64].

The concept of proto-industrialization is a contribution to the long debate on the origins of the industrial revolution and, more generally, on the genesis of industrial capitalism. In the fashion of the time the concept is sometimes given a quasi-scientific status by its proponents who refer to it as a model. When historians use the word 'model' in preference to the more old-fashioned 'hypothesis' they have two objectives in mind. First, they are simply coining a descriptive label to fasten on to a bundle of historial events. All students of economic history are familiar with such labels as 'industrial revolution' and 'capitalism'; although often the first faltering step to wisdom is the realization that identical labels can mean different things to different historians [see 17; 41]. The second purpose of a model is to provide a set of generalized explanations of historical developments. This is done by observing regularities in the data and then, by a process of induction, establishing reasons for them.

In the present case proto-industrialization is concerned with the fact that in Europe before the industrial revolution manufacturing industries supplying national and international markets were often located in the countryside. Production was organized in cottage workshops where men, women and children combined the manufacture of textiles, leather goods, metal wares and similar items with farming. Not all industry, of course, was organized in this way. This form of organization was not found, for example, in the mining or metal-smelting industries, or in activities such as milling or tanning which required a relatively large investment in fixed capital. There were also dozens and scores of full-time craftsmen in every market town producing clothing, household goods, saddlery, pots and pans, and the like, for the local market. Nevertheless there were many regions of Europe where cottage workers combined the production of industrial goods, overwhelmingly textiles, with the cultivation of the soil or the grazing of sheep and cattle. The essence of cottage industries was that labour employed in this manner was cheap; therefore the goods produced were competitive in national and international markets.

As a description, therefore, proto-industrialization points to a common feature of the economy of pre-industrial Europe: the existence of industries in the countryside. In its dynamic, or explanatory, aspect proto-industrialization postulates that cottage industries contained the conditions for the eventual development of factory-based industries; it analyses the way in which during the eighteenth and nineteenth centuries the factory system grew out of rural industry. It is because cottage industry preceded and sometimes led on to modern industry that it has been labelled proto-industry, that is, 'the first phase of industrialization'. In some instances, however, the second phase did not occur and instead rural industry decayed, so producing 'deindustrialization'.

Proto-industrialization also explores other aspects of industrial development. For example, considerable attention is paid to 'proletarianization' whereby once independent farmer-manufacturers were turned into wage-earners as a result of their increasing reliance on merchant-capitalists who supplied them with raw materials and who bought their manufactured goods for resale in distant markets. Accompanying proletarianization was 'immiseration', said to afflict cottage workers as they were metamorphized into wage workers, thereby suffering a fall in their social and economic status and spending their miserable earnings on alcohol and other debasing consumption goods. Finally, proto-industrialization suggests that the growth of cottage industry and its eventual evolution into factory industry affected the formation, size, structure and functioning of households and families, and the rate of population growth, a theme that by some oversight has failed to be christened 'socialization'.

Historical models can be used as research tools to point to issues that are worth investigating. Proto-industrialization has initiated comprehensive studies of rural industries geared to distant markets in eighteenth and nineteenth-century Europe and also elsewhere as scholars have come to appreciate that they were not purely a European phenomenon [see 28; 75]. Bolder spirits among historians also claim that the concept of proto-industrialization does more than merely reveal facets of the past. It also contains lessons for those interested in strategies of economic development at the present time and in the future. As Charles and Richard Tilly have written, 'our eventual hope is to specify the relevance and irrelevance of European history both for general theories of economic development and for projections of economic change in contemporary countries' [89, *195*].

As we have remarked, proto-industrialization and its attendant neologisms are part of the study of the development of industrial civilization. When Arnold Toynbee delivered his lectures in 1880–1 on the industrial revolution in England, so launching the phrase into the stream of historical consciousness, he treated it as an almost complete break with the past: 'the essence of the industrial revolution [was] the substitution of competition for the medieval regulation which had previously controlled the production and distribution of wealth'. In its more narrowly manufacturing aspects, 'the all-prominent fact ... [of the industrial revolution was] the substitution of the factory for the domestic system' [91, *58, 63*]. The point was put even more dramatically by Charles Beard in 1901 when he wrote that 'suddenly, almost like a thunderbolt from a clear sky, were ushered in the storm and stress of the Industrial Revolution' [quoted 30, *3*].

Such an explosive interpretation of industrial development was unlikely to survive the erosion of empirical research, and it was eventually replaced by a story of slow evolution. Two works more than any others established a more gradualist view into the historiography of the industrial revolution. In 1926 the first volume of Sir John Clapham's *An Economic History of Modern Britain* demonstrated how incomplete industrialization was by 1830 when 'the country [still] abounded in ancient types of industrial organization and in transitional types of all variety' [15, *I, 143*]. Even more influential was T. S. Ashton's *The Industrial Revolution, 1760–1830* (1948) which summed up a generation of historical research by pointing out that 'the system of human relationships that is sometimes called capitalism had its origins long before 1760, and attained its full development long after 1830; there is a danger of overlooking the essential fact of continuity' [3, *2*].

At about the same time as Clapham was writing an alternative picture of industrial development was being painted, primarily in the works of J. U. Nef. In a massive book on the British coal industry published in 1932 he wrote that 'the late sixteenth and seventeenth centuries may have been marked by an industrial revolution only less important than that which began towards the end of the eighteenth century' [72, *I*, *165*]. In successive publications his tentative industrial revolution of the sixteenth and seventeenth centuries hardened into an event 'no less' important than its more famous successor, and other authors have added to it a series of revolutions stretching from the Bronze Age to the twentieth century [see 17].

The concept of proto-industrialization has little in common with views of economic development as a series of revolutions. It is more akin to the evolutionary tradition but it differs from it in one important respect: it sees earlier forms of industry, not merely as preceding factory industry, but as being causally related to it. As such it has affinities with various 'stage' theories of economic development that were propounded first by the German historical economists writing between the 1840s and the First World War. Although differing from one another on points of detail, all stressed the importance of the economic changes taking place during the sixteenth, seventeenth and eighteenth centuries in laying the foundations of industrial society in the nineteenth [see 45]. Much later, W. W. Rostow revived the stage approach and identified five stages of economic growth, of which two – the 'pre-conditions for take-off', and the 'take-off' proper – approximate to the phases of proto-industry and factory industry [80; 81]. Mendels, the main begetter of proto-industrialization, however, might protest that his model is more specific than Rostow's in explaining how one stage leads to the next.

Proto-industrialization also has points of similarity with that other German tradition, of Marxist writings dealing with the transition from feudalism to capitalism. One of the most influential publications of this kind in English has been Maurice Dobb's *Studies in the Development of Capitalism* (1946). The crucial stages of development according to the Marxist model are the feudal mode of production which disintegrated during the fifteenth and sixteenth centuries, and the 'definite triumph of capitalism at the end of the eighteenth century' [43, *162*]. Between these two stages existed an indeterminate period described by Dobb as 'an early and still immature stage of Capitalism' during which 'capital began to penetrate production on a considerable scale, either in the form of a fairly matured relationship between capitalist and hired wage-earners or in the less developed form of the subordination of domestic handicraftsmen, working in their own homes, to a capitalist on the so-called "putting-out system"' [29, *18, 19*].

Without using the word, Dobb was outlining the proto-industrial stage of industry and it is not surprising that recent Marxist writers have adopted the concept with enthusiasm. Thus, the editors of a recent volume devoted to *Industrialization before Industrialization* claim that 'proto-industrialization ... belonged to the second phase of the great transformation from feudalism to capitalism. It was indeed one of the driving forces during this second phase' [54, *7*]. As if to emphasize its affinity to the Marxist scheme, one of the contributors, Peter Kriedte, refers to 'a crisis in the proto-industrial mode of production' that caused this first phase of industry to give way to the second, just as the 'crisis in the feudal mode of production' in the Marxist model propelled society from feudalism to capitalism [54, *137*]. There are differences, of course. The literature on proto-industry has concentrated on the eighteenth and nineteenth centuries whereas Marxists range much more widely. More important, the Marxist debate has had little to say about the connexions between industrialization and population growth [see 40], a theme central to proto-industrialization, although recently there has been some attempt to incorporate demography into Marxist explanations of long-run economic change [see 83]. On the whole, though, Marxists put much greater stress on class relationships as a cause of economic change [see 12]. In the proto-industrial literature, on the other hand, class relationships are treated more as the outcome of industrial developments.

Historical models, like industrial revolutions, rarely appear like thunderbolts from a clear sky but have their antecedents in earlier writings. Before Mendels explicitly formulated the features of proto-industrialization in 1972 they had been foreshadowed in a number of articles. In 1961 Joan Thirsk published an important essay in which she drew attention to 'semi-farming, semi-industrial communities' supplying national and international markets with textiles. Their common feature was that they possessed abundant supplies of labour, although she explicitly denied any intention of propounding 'a theory for the situation of rural handicraft industries which can be applied mechanistically to them all' [87, *86*]. At about the same time Rudolph Braun in a study of eighteenth-century Switzerland traced the effects that the introduction of cottage industry had on the process of family formation in agrarian communities [10].

13

A little later E. L. Jones pointed to the regional specialization developing within European agriculture from the later seventeenth century whereby some districts devoted themselves to the commercial production of cereals, while 'less-favoured areas tended to concentrate on livestock production and to switch into rural industry' [50, *138–9*]. Finally, in 1969 D. C. Coleman, writing of the development of new drapery production in England at the end of the sixteenth century, referred to 'a commercialization of peasant techniques' whereby cheap fabrics once made by farmers for their own use were now manufactured to satisfy the demands of expanding international markets [18, *421*]. All the elements of 'industrialization before the factory system' existed in print before Mendels finally fitted them together into a generalized account of industrial development.

Just why proto-industrialization was finally constructed in the early 1970s is a matter of speculation. The knowledge of rural industries was hardly new; they had been discussed at length, for example, by the pioneer English historians, Cunningham and Unwin, a century ago [26; 93], as well as by the German historical economists from whom they drew much of their inspiration. The decisive difference in the 1970s was probably that rural industries were now being studied by scholars trained in economics and familiar with concepts developed to analyse the workings of labour markets in agrarian-based economies [see 48; 59]. Such scholars shared an interest in the problems of promoting growth in present-day underdeveloped countries. A knowledge of how proto-industries were transformed into factory industries in western Europe in the eighteenth and nineteenth centuries would, they hoped, demonstrate how the process might be repeated today. The model of proto-industrialization was thus the creation of economically-trained historians. They were not, moreover, simply borrowing the economists' tools, but were attempting to forge new ones helpful to the understanding of present-day and future economic development [see 70, *xiii–xiv*]. Just how successful they have been we shall be better able to judge when we have considered the component parts of the model.

2 The Features of Proto-industry

Before the industrial revolution there existed throughout Europe a myriad of small workshops producing basic consumer goods. They were located mostly in towns where they catered for the demands of the local urban population and the agrarian community of the surrounding countryside, and included the tailors, dressmakers, shoemakers, bakers, butchers, carpenters, braziers and others, who made up a quarter or a third of the working population of pre-industrial towns. Some craftsmen – tanners, blacksmiths and the like – also worked in the countryside where their activities complemented those of local farmers. Here and there, too, were dotted larger-scale units of production in such processes as iron-smelting, corn-milling and paper-making where capital requirements and technical skills extended beyond the resources of cottage workshops [see 19].

None of these activities would be recognised as examples of proto-industry by the proponents of the concept since their markets were local and they did not evolve into factory production. Rather, proto-industrialization was, in the words of Mendels, 'a first phase [of industrialization] which preceded and prepared modern industrialization proper' [64, *241*].

Proto-industries were marked by four features which, in the right circumstances, led to the development of factory-based industry. First, proto-industrial craftsmen produced goods for markets beyond the regions where they lived; often these markets were overseas and the products of one region competed with the products of another. Second, the industrial products were made by peasant-manufacturers who combined, say, weaving or stocking-knitting with farming. Manufacturing slotted into the slack periods of the farming year, and it fitted in particularly well with pastoral farming which was less labour-intensive than corn-growing. Labour employed in this way was cheap since, in the absence of industry, farmers and their families would be idle for part of the year. In the language of economics, the opportunity costs of the labour of peasant-manufacturers were low. Cottage industry also made minimal demands on fixed capital, for no special industrial premises were required and the machinery used –

15

spinning wheels, looms and anvils, for example – was usually small and inexpensive: small enough to be housed in domestic cottages and cheap enough to be owned by poor farmers. Relatively expensive machines such as stocking-knitting frames were sometimes rented but in general industries requiring large and expensive equipment were not suited to a domestic form of organization. Neither were processes using materials of high value such as gold and silver.

The third important characteristic of proto-industrialization, it is argued, was that rural manufacturing stimulated commercial farming by creating a market for food. Proto-industrial workers did not grow enough food for their own needs, either because their farms were too small or too barren to begin with, or because manufacturing expanded to take up so much of their time that they neglected their farms. They were therefore obliged to buy supplies from other producers. This brings us to the fourth feature of proto-industrialization. Towns located in manufacturing zones were principally centres of trade and commerce. The merchants who supplied raw materials to cottage manufacturers lived in towns, and finishing processes – the dyeing of woollen cloth, for example – were sometimes carried out there by skilled workmen. Weekly or bi-weekly markets were held in towns and were attended by merchants who came to buy manufactured goods for export, and also by farmers and dealers who travelled from districts of commercial farming to sell their produce.

Regions of proto-industry were extensive throughout eighteenth-century Europe: for example, 'in Maine, Picardy, and Languedoc in France, Westphalia, Silesia, and southern Saxony in Germany, Flanders and Twente in the Low Countries, Ulster, the West Riding, the Cotswolds and East Anglia in Great Britain and many more' [27, *105*; see also 52; 76]. The cloth industries – wool, linen, cotton and silk – were the most important of the proto-industrial crafts. Textile production had been widespread throughout the economy of Europe in the middle ages and early-modern period, but from the later seventeenth century regional specialization became more pronounced. Thus the first of the features of proto-industrialization emerged.

The reason for the greater development of proto-industrial zones in the century or so before the industrial revolution was that market conditions were altering [see 50]. They were changing because within Europe population that had been growing from the end of the fifteenth century had now ceased to increase, so causing a widespread sluggishness in demand for basic consumer goods such as textiles. At the same time, though, new market opportunities were opening up outside Europe in areas of overseas settlement [see 42]. Both developments placed a premium on inexpensive products: within Europe as merchants struggled to maintain or even increase sales in stagnant markets by selling cheaper goods; outside Europe because demand was concentrated on lower-value products. Since labour was the largest element in the cost of manufacturing textiles and many other products, merchants sought out goods that had been made by the cheapest available labour. Those regions of the countryside possessing supplies of labour in excess of the requirements of agriculture were well placed to take advantage of these opportunities that changing market conditions afforded.

This part of the proto-industrialization thesis can be illustrated by the example of the West Riding of Yorkshire. Cheap woollen cloths had been made in the region from at least the fifteenth century, principally for the home market, and in 1700 the West Riding produced roughly one-fifth of total English cloth output. As an exporting district, however, it had been overshadowed by the Wiltshire-Gloucestershire woollen industry and by East Anglia. During the eighteenth century the position changed dramatically. Total English production doubled or trebled, but in the West Riding output rose eightfold, the greater part of the increase occurring in worsteds, the manufacture of which was concentrated in the north-west of the Riding. The production of traditional woollen cloths also rose, chiefly in the south-eastern parts of the district. Cloth was now produced chiefly for the export market, the West Riding having advantages over the older exporting regions of the West of England and East Anglia. These advantages may have included lower labour costs – the literature is not conclusive on this point – but some weight also has to be attached to the many varieties of cloths produced, adapted to the requirements of particular markets, and to the entrepreneurial skills and superior organization of producers in the region [see 37; 47; 95].

An even more striking example of an export-led expansion of a rurally located textile industry occurred in Ireland during the eighteenth century. Poor-quality linens for domestic consumption had been made in Ireland for centuries, but at the end of the seventeenth century an influx of English and continental expertise into the province of Ulster, coupled with the opening up of the

English market to Irish producers, resulted in a commercialization of traditional techniques and an improvement in quality. From insignificant levels at the beginning of the eighteenth century, linen cloth exports rose to over 40 million yards by 1800. The bulk of the output came from farmer-weavers living in parts of the Ulster countryside. As a contemporary wrote in 1819:

> it is not at all necessary to the advancement of that trade [i.e. linen], that either the spinners or the weavers should be collected into overgrown cities, or congregated into crowded and unwholesome factories. Those branches of the linen business, which are their particular concern, can be perfectly well managed in their respective cabins. [84, *467*]

According to an estimate made in 1770 there were then 42,000 weavers in Ulster. Taking account of household members also involved in linen production, as many as 200,000 persons may have been connected with the industry, the equivalent to a quarter of the province's population [24; 25; 32].

Turning to continental Europe, the spinning and weaving of flax developed as important activities in Flanders during the eighteenth century, displacing an older woollen industry. The linen-manufacturing zone lay in the interior of the country and was bounded on the west by a coastal strip devoted to commercial farming, and to the east by an area specializing in the cultivation of flax used by the linen manufacturers. The growth of output during the eighteenth century was less spectacular than in Ulster during the same period, but the proportion of the population employed in the linen industry – nearly all of them living in the countryside – was greater. More than 80 per cent of output was exported, much of it to Spain and the Spanish-American colonies. In the words of Mendels, 'the economic history of Flanders from the late seventeenth to the late eighteenth century adequately fits...a phase of "proto-industrialization"' [65, *203*].

In Germany the Rhineland offers a different example of rural industry. The area bounded by Krefeld, Aachen, Cologne and the Wupper valley was a mixed textile and metal-working zone producing mainly silks around Krefeld, woollens in the vicinity of Aachen, and linen, silks and cottons in the Wupper valley. The textile crafts were not exclusively rural, but during the eighteenth century the most rapid expansion occurred in those branches of production supplying distant markets and employing cheap country labour. Around Krefeld, for example, 'a thriving silk industry had taken root. Drawing upon the labour of underemployed linen weavers in the vicinity it was able to keep costs low and thus successfully compete in foreign markets.' Similarly, at the end of the seventeenth century the woollen industry in the city of Aachen had broken loose of restrictions imposed by urban gilds and was spreading into the countryside. The outcome of the developments was that:

> on the eve of the French Revolution the lower Rhine textile trades had become an integral part of the 'Atlantic economy' and fully shared the benefits of its buoyancy. Low costs of production, making it possible to meet the challenge of foreign competition, assured the industries of the region this favourable position. [53, 557; see also 6]

The cases cited so far refer to textiles, and the literature of proto-industrialization generally is dominated by discussions of woollens and linen. Rural industry, though, was not confined to textiles. In England, for instance, there were two important metal-working zones in the later seventeenth and eighteenth centuries that have some claim to be regarded as 'proto-industrial' in that they employed part-time agricultural labour, produced for export markets, and eventually became centres of factory production. In the vicinity of Walsall and Birmingham in the West Midlands a considerable proportion of the rural population combined farming with the manufacture of nails, knives, scythes, locks and the like. Much of the output was destined for the American market where the log cabins of the frontiersmen were fastened together by Birmingham nails. Similarly, in the Sheffield region of south Yorkshire knives, scythes and cutlery were manufactured for export by 'farmer-craftsmen [who] followed a dual occupation combining agriculture and metal-working' [38, 18; see also 23; 82). On the Continent there were important metal-working regions in the Liège Basin and the Rhineland.

The model of proto-industrialization stresses that the labour of peasant-manufacturers was cheap, although we should note in passing that very often in the literature this cheapness is assumed rather than demonstrated empirically. There has been considerable discussion, however, of why country-based labour was low-cost labour. In towns competing demands by employers pushed up wages; and in the case of self-employed craftsmen, gild restrictions on recruitment into the crafts they controlled served to keep the price of labour high. Rural labour was cheaper because there industrial production was undertaken by workers who would otherwise be periodically underemployed. Nevertheless, rural labour was not equally cheap in all regions and proto-industry therefore was not found everywhere in the countryside. Even within a particular proto-industrial zone, manufacturing was unevenly distributed: the populations of some parishes might be heavily involved with industry and in others hardly at all.

Joan Thirsk has noted three conditions that could result in supplies of cheap labour in a region. First, she suggests that low-cost labour was more likely to be found in pastoral regions than in areas of cereal farming with their more intensive demand for labour. Second, underemployed, and therefore cheap, farm labour was commonly available in communities composed of small freeholders living in areas unfettered by manorial control. In those villages where manor courts exercised a strict supervision of tenures – by, for example, preventing the subdivision of farms – and restricted the settlement of newcomers in the village, there was little likelihood that a labour supply in excess of the requirements of agriculture would emerge to any great extent. But where manorial control was weak or absent, farms were often subdivided; and where there were no community restrictions on immigration the population was likely to grow and outrun the employment opportunities available locally in agriculture. Finally, cheap labour was prevalent in upland and moorland districts with infertile soils and extensive commons. Such regions tended to become overpopulated, partly because the land was too barren to support a large population by arable farming to begin with, but also because the very availability of extensive grazing land – married to an absence of weak community controls on settlement – attracted emigrants from elsewhere [87].

Thirsk supports her general propositions by evidence drawn from several English textile regions. Thus, in Wiltshire, Gloucestershire and Somerset, textile manufacture was concentrated in the dairying regions but was unimportant in the sheep-corn areas. In Suffolk, similarly, cloth production was located mainly in the dairying district of the county. This was the wood-pasture region to the south where manorial organization was weak. Turning to Kent, there had been a vigorous textile industry in the seventeenth century concentrated in the Weald, a heavily populated pastoral region, although it was in decline during the eighteenth. Further north, Westmorland, a county of mountain and moor, was a considerable producer of coarse woollen cloth and knitted stockings, the labour coming from the densely populated lowland valleys. In the dales bordering Westmorland and north Yorkshire farming communities eked out a precarious existence by combining the grazing of cattle and sheep with hand knitting woollen hosiery for the London market.

Some other English studies confirm Thirsk's generalizations. To cite just one, about one-third of the West Riding of Yorkshire was composed of upland grazing and was inhabited by numerous small freeholders who combined subsistence farming with the manufacture of worsteds. Near to the market towns the farms were generally more fertile and their occupants were occupied with the production of food and with weaving woollen cloths. Finally, to the east of the Riding there was an area of tillage where industry was unimportant and the main purpose of agriculture was growing grain for the textile districts [47].

An association between proto-industrialization and regions of pastoral farming or infertile soils as suggested by proponents of the concept thus seems well-founded [see 66]. Nevertheless, it was not the only possible relationship and there are examples of rural industry concentrated in areas more concerned with cereal farming than with pasture or rough grazing. In Ulster, for example, County Armagh was at the very heart of the linen-producing zone, but 'notwithstanding the minute subdivision of land which is the natural result of these peculiar circumstances [i.e. linen manufacture] the farmers ... are more than competent to supply its population with vegetable [i.e. cereals and potatoes], though not with animal food ...' [84, 467]. Cultivation, though, was often neglected in favour of linen weaving and Arthur Young remarked that the county displayed 'the worst husbandry I have met with' [97, I, 127]. We can hardly argue that the opportunity costs of the labour of farmers who neglected their fields to concentrate on weaving were negligible, but their priorities were economically rational since they were an attempt to maximize family income. On the Continent, to take another example, the Pays de Caux in Upper Normandy was a crop-growing area which from the 1720s developed an extensive rurally-located cotton industry.

Manufacturing was organized by cotton merchants based in Rouen and it provided a large number of landless people in the Caux with a valuable supplement to the incomes they earned as agricultural labourers [see 34].

The importance of social structure in influencing the geographical distribution of rural industry can be illustrated by the example of framework-knitting (i.e. the manufacture of woollen hosiery on knitting frames) in late seventeenth and eighteenth-century Leicestershire. The crucial social distinction was between 'open' and 'closed' parishes. Framework-knitting was located mainly in the former where the land was occupied by a large number of small cultivators who needed an industrial activity to supplement their meagre agricultural incomes; some cultivators even mortgaged their farms to raise money to buy a stocking frame. Before the mid-eighteenth century stocking knitters were usually independent producers, but as the population grew in the parishes devoted to knitting, there emerged a class of poor men who were unable to afford frames and who therefore worked for already established knitters or for merchants who supplied them with yarn and from whom they rented knitting frames. By contrast, in the 'closed' parishes the land was owned by a few large landlords who leased out their estates in large farms which were devoted to commercial farming. The landlords paid the poor rate and they therefore placed strict controls on cottage building, permitting their tenant farmers to erect only as many as necessary to house essential farm labourers. In the absence of housing and alternative employments, landless labourers in the closed parishes faced the choice of working for large farmers or moving away from the parish. Some went to the open parishes in search of employment in the knitting industry [see 58; 67].

The behaviour of landlords in the closed parishes of Leicestershire contrasts with that of landlords in the linen zones of Ulster, Silesia and Flanders. In the former farmer-weavers normally leased their farms from landlords but they were subject to very little regulation in matters of subdivision, cottage building, or farming practices. However, landlords encouraged linen production by establishing markets so that their tenants could earn money to pay the rent. In Silesia, which was still largely feudal in the eighteenth century, landlords were happy for their tenants to take up weaving so that they could afford the many feudal obligations heaped upon them [53]. In Flanders, landlords in the linen regions encouraged their tenants to subdivide holdings as a way of increasing their total rent incomes [9].

There is a common assumption in the literature of proto-industrialization that peasant-manufacturers were, or soon became, wage-earners employed by capitalist merchants who supplied them with raw materials to process in their own cottages, nevertheless retaining ownership of the materials throughout the various stages of manufacture. But this was only one possibility. Another was that peasant-manufacturers were self-employed craftsmen growing or buying their own raw materials and selling their finished goods to dealers who, in turn, dispatched them to their final destinations. We must not push the distinction between a self-employed craftsman and a wage-earner too far, however, for a man could be both simultaneously; or he might be independent at one point in time and an employee at another. As Ramsay [77] and others have pointed out, relations between manufacturers and dealers before the industrial revolution took many forms that defy modern categories of employer and employee. It is a criticism of the proto-industrialization model that 'the immense variety of organisational and industrial structures is ignored and the corresponding diversity of accumulation and change is glossed over' [47, 37].

Some examples will demonstrate the complexities. In the West Riding woollen industry the typical producer in the eighteenth century was a self-employed farmer-weaver who owned his own tools, grew his own wool, or purchased it locally, and sold his output to dealers who travelled around the urban cloth markets. In the worsted branch of the industry, by contrast, spinners and weavers were usually employees of merchant clothiers. In Ulster most linen producers were independent farmer-weavers who grew flax on their own farms which was harvested and prepared by family labour, spun by the women and woven by the men. Weavers with insufficient flax could buy it, or yarn, from the many petty dealers who visited the linen markets. These same markets were attended by drapers and bleachers who bought the linen webs and prepared them for the final markets. In the words of Stuart, writing in 1819, weavers were not employees but 'free agents whose employments are diversified and rational' [84, 467]. Only towards the end of the century did a class of wage-earning weavers emerge. On the Continent most linen weavers appear to have been self-employed, although wage-earners were widespread in the woollen and metal crafts. In the metal-working trades in the English West

Midlands self-employed workers and wage-earners were both common, with the former predominating among the more prosperous scythe-makers and the latter among poor nailers (32; 47; 53; 65; 82].

Just as the proto-industrialization literature glosses over the many variations in organization, so it provides no very convincing explanation of *why* some peasant manufacturers were self-employed and others were wage-earners. The most ingenious reason is that offered by Millward who suggests that wage-labour emerged under two conditions. The first is 'when there is a demand for high volumes of standardized middle-quality products'. The second is where 'there was a distinct innovation in the mix of materials [e.g. the new draperies]' [68, 28–9]. In these circumstances, Millward argues, merchants found it easier to obtain the quantities and qualities of goods they required in order to satisfy demand by supplying employees with raw materials than by buying manufactured wares from large numbers of self-employed craftsmen. The argument works well enough for, say, worsteds and metal-wares where the volume of demand was high and there was a large variety in the types and qualities of goods produced. But this was true, too, with linen and woollens which were often made by independent producers. Some additional explanation is called for. It is noticeable that it was often the most impoverished producers who became wage-earners: those too poor to buy raw materials and in need of an industrial wage for their subsistence.

In Marxist literature on capitalist development there is an arcane debate on whether 'a section of producers themselves accumulated capital and took to trade', or whether 'a section of the existing merchant class began to "take possession directly of the means of production"' [29, 123; 85, 52–6]. The proponents of the concept of proto-industrialization do not have much to say explicitly on this subject, perhaps because empirical studies of rural industries suggest a complex set of arrangements that cannot easily be generalized. Throughout southern England, as Ramsay has pointed out, the cloth export trade from the sixteenth century was dominated by London and the important figure in trade was the clothier. He might own a loom or two, he probably put out materials to spinners and weavers in their own cottages, but 'his crucial responsibility lay in the delivery of the cloth to the London market and finding a purchaser there' [77, 23]. Clothiers lived among the weavers and spinners and may well have evolved from their ranks. In the West Midlands nail trade, also, marketing enterprise seems to have developed initially within the region although as a substantial trade grew up with the American end of the business it increasingly passed into the hands of London-based ironmongers and merchants [23]. But there are also examples of external interests coming into a region seeking out manufactured goods for export. In Ulster, for example, linen production was harnessed to overseas markets by English settlers and landlords [24; 25]; in Silesia, also, locally produced linen was bought by merchants who came from elsewhere [53]. Turning to a different trade, London-based merchants sent their agents into the English East Midlands to buy footwear and hosiery more cheaply than they could get them in the capital [13].

As we have noted, proto-industrialization postulates that rural industry develops in association with commercial agriculture. Commercial farming and rural manufacturing were, in fact, often found in close proximity. In Wiltshire, for example, there were two distinct but contiguous farming regions: 'the enclosed, non-manorial countries – the cheese and butter countries – [which] were the lands of family farmers and self-employed persons', and 'the manorialized, champion, sheep-and-corn countries ... [which] were the main field for the development of agrarian capitalism and for the agricultural revolution' [quoted 87, 74]. The former was the home of cloth manufacturers and the latter of commercial farmers. In Ulster, where much of the linen zone was a fertile region, weavers and farmers lived cheek-by-jowl. Nevertheless, much of the food consumed by linen manufacturers came from 'great importations' from other parts of Ireland, 'besides what comes occasionally from England and Scotland' [97, I, 133].

Proto-industrialization draws a clear distinction between countryside and town: manufacturing was done principally in the former, with the latter being centres of trade and commerce. The functions of towns are well illustrated by the example of Ulster where, in the late eighteenth century, there were about sixty places scattered throughout the province serving as weekly linen markets. Most were small and the bulk of trade was concentrated in the three major towns of Armagh, Lisburn and Lurgan. From there cloths were dispatched to the bleach yards before being transported to Dublin, Newry, Belfast or Londonderry for export [32]. Similarly, in the West Riding of Yorkshire, 'the eighteenth century towns, especially the smaller ones, functioned chiefly as trading centres. Such towns as Dent, Bedale, Skipton, Cawood, Aberford, and the like spent the greater part of the year in slumber, only awakening for the annual fairs or the more frequent market-days' [37, *385*]. A few strategically placed centres grew to larger importance: Wakefield from the mid-seventeenth century; Leeds from the end of the seventeenth century, with growing competition from Halifax and Huddersfield during the eighteenth. On the Continent, the towns in Flanders actually decayed as manufacturing centres during the eighteenth century at the same time as they increased their concentration on the marketing of cloth. Thus, the number of looms at work in Ghent fell by 25 per cent between 1700 and 1780, but the quantity of linen passing through the Ghent market doubled in the same period [65].

Ultimately, the dichotomy between urban and rural industry perceived by historians of proto-industrialization is somewhat strained, unless 'urban' is interpreted in a strictly legalistic sense to mean a place possessing borough status [see 'Introduction' to 8]. It may be generally true that before the industrial revolution towns were primarily centres of trade and distribution. Nevertheless, they also contained a fair sprinkling of industrial workers, some of whom were employed in a very similar fashion to rural craftsmen. The Ulster town of Lisburn, for example, was the home of skilled damask weavers working on complex looms too large to be accommodated in rural cottages. There were also a large number of spinners and plain linen weavers working in their own homes [16]. In England the best known example of a city possessing a substantial textile industry in the seventeenth and eighteenth centuries is Norwich [see 22]. Conversely, there were rural communities – such as Shepshed in Leicestershire with its heavy commitment to framework-knitting – that became so involved in manufacturing during the eighteenth century that they became *de facto* urban centres [see 58].

To sum up, the essence of proto-industrialization was that industries producing for export markets became established in regions of the countryside possessing supplies of cheap labour. The workers might be self-employed or they might be wage-earners working for town-based capitalists; in either case the home was the workshop and the household the unit of production. A further characteristic of proto-industrialization was the interdependence of zones of rural industry and zones of commercial farming. The dynamic of proto-industrialization was provided by the force of the market: without the stimulus of large and competitive markets, rural manufacturers vegetated quietly in the countryside, supplying household and local needs, but untroubled by the pressures of commercial capitalism. In some regions the demands of the market became so strong that manufacturing outstripped the available labour supply, so inducing changes in industrial organization and techniques. Proto-industry was then transformed into the second stage of modern, factory based, industry. The transformation did not take place everywhere, however; some rural-industrial zones instead slipped gently into obscurity. To the problems of industrialization and deindustrialization we now turn.

3 Industrialization and Deindustrialization

Why and how did cottage industry become metamorphized into modern factory industry? According to Mendels [64] there were five links between the first and second stages of industrialization.

The most important was that industries in the countryside became the victims of their own success. The prime reason for their development in the first place was the low cost of labour arising from the widespread underemployment in certain types of agrarian economies. However, supplies of labour were not totally elastic. As increasing numbers of cultivators moved into manufacturing – or devoted a larger part of their time to industry and a lesser part to farming – so the productivity and hence the earnings of those remaining in agriculture rose. It now cost more to entice them into industry; in economic terms, their opportunity costs had increased.

There is a logical difficulty at this point because the concept of proto-industrialization postulates that cottage industry stimulated the growth of population and hence of the labour supply (see Chapter 4). So an assumption must be made that the demand for labour eventually grew more rapidly than its supply. Faced with rising labour costs, merchants and employers cast their net over ever widening areas. This had the further effect of increasing distribution and supervision costs, and there came a point where it was cheaper to reorganize production methods and employ labour in centralized workshops where it could be supervised and also to devise or introduce machinery which would raise the productivity of labour.

Production in centralized workshops was more capital-intensive than cottage production. Buildings were needed to accommodate the machinery that had once competed for space with bed and board in farm cottages and to house the workforce. Centralized workshops contained more elaborate machinery, perhaps powered by a water wheel or a steam engine, developed to replace the labour that had become too expensive, so adding to the demands for capital. This brings us to the second link between the first and second stages of industry outlined by the model: the capital came from the proto-industrial merchants. As Mendels puts it, 'proto-industrialization had created an accumulation of capital in the hands of merchant employers, making possible the adoption of machine industry with its (relatively) higher capital costs' [64, *244*]. These same merchants also possessed marketing and managerial skills that carried over into the conduct of factory industry, thus creating the third link between proto-industry and modern industrialization.

There were two further connections. Within cottage industry there was, according to Mendels, a reservoir of technical knowledge that could be adapted to modern industry: 'many of the machine builders of the industrial revolution in England had been trained in the old handicraft industrial sectors and they were in intimate contact with the scientific advances of the time' [64, *244*]. Finally, with the development of factories and an urbanized labour force, for whom a corn field or a cow were merely objects within a dimming folk memory, the old association between areas of proto-industry and regions of commercial agriculture became more vital than ever.

Proto-industrialization as originally formulated makes no claim that cottage industry prepared workers for the rigours of factory life, although the suggestion appears in Marxist elaborations. There are two reasons for its absence in the original version, one theoretical and one empirical. Modern factory industry produces goods by a combination of fixed capital and labour and, as Mokyr points out, 'it is immaterial whether the workers who become the urban proletariat came originally from the rural-industrial ... sector or were most active in agriculture' [70, *134–5*]. This observation carries with it the important implication that modern factory industry did *not* always grow out of cottage industry.

As far as the empirical evidence is concerned, it is abundantly clear that in England, to take but one example, rural-industrial workers possessed irregular working habits, with a particular predeliction for St Monday as well as the more ecclesiastically recognized holy days; and that they were far from amenable to the regular work discipline of the factories. In the metal-working industries of the West Midlands Monday continued to be observed as a holiday until the third quarter of the nineteenth century despite the attempts of employers to end the practice [see 4, 78]. This is not to deny that one-time cottage workers were recruited into the factories in the late eighteenth and early nineteenth centuries, but it was economic circumstances, not prior experience of industrial work, that led them there.

Of the five suggested links between proto-industry and factory industry the greatest difficulties of verification are raised by the first. Again using the example of England, there are several reasons for believing that labour became more expensive over the course of much of the eighteenth century. The estimates of Wrigley and Schofield show that until the 1770s population generally grew at less than 0.6 per cent per annum, which, given the level of demand for labour, meant that real wages were either constant or were rising. Only when the rate of growth of population accelerated in the last three decades of the century do real wages, nationally, appear to have fallen [57]. Even then it is probable that real wages continued to increase in the most rapidly industrializing parts of the country where there was a large demand for labour; in these regions there were many complaints from manufacturers about the shortage and expense of labour [see 4; 5; 31]. The organizational changes and technical innovations taking place in English industry in the later eighteenth century therefore did so against a background of rising labour costs in some industries; but this is some way from proving that particular entrepreneurs reacted to mounting wage bills by changing their methods of production.

The most systematic investigation of the operation of labour markets during the period of industrialization is Mokyr's study of the Low Countries. He draws a distinction between the northern provinces that eventually formed the Netherlands, and the southern provinces that eventually became Belgium. The economy of the former was characterized by a concentration on trade and maritime activities; it possessed a highly commercialized agricultural sector and the general level of wages was high. The industrial sector was small and stagnating in the late eighteenth and early nineteenth centuries. Belgium, by contrast, possessed extensive rural industries producing woollens, linens and metal-wares, a rapidly growing population and low wages; and during the early decades of the nineteenth century it successfully made the transition from proto-industry to modern factory industry. In the Low Countries, therefore, the association between high wages and industrial innovation was the reverse of the relationship in England. Mokyr's explanation is that in the Netherlands high wages cut into profits; and since profits were the main source of capital, entrepreneurs could not afford to introduce capital-intensive methods of production. In Belgium there was no such problem. English textile machinery was introduced because its productivity gains, compared with traditional labour-intensive methods, were great, and it was financed by the profits that the cheap labour had made possible [70].

This analysis compels a reassessment of the English experience. If high wages inhibited industrial development in the Netherlands, why did they not also act as a barrier to development in England? Perhaps the most plausible answer to this question is that industrialization occurred earlier in England; the first generation of machines was relatively cheap in capital terms and to some extent the initial costs of development could be offset by savings in working capital and distribution costs. Once installed, new machines yielded to their innovators a quasi-rent that financed the next round of development; that is to say, the earnings of one machine, over and above its operating costs, could be transferred to meet the costs of a new and technically superior machine. In practical terms, we may envisage cotton spinners moving through a hierarchy of machinery from spinning wheels to jennies, to water-frames, to steam-powered mules, each more expensive but more productive than the last. A similar argument applies to centralized workshops initially housing traditional machinery. Their cost savings, compared with dispersed cottage production, could be used to finance the introduction of labour-saving machinery. Hence, in England, high wages were a stimulus to innovation, and the capital costs of new machinery were not a hindrance because they rose only gradually. In the Low Countries, on the other hand, industrialization came later and was based on imported English machinery; investment was more 'lumpy' and needed the prior accumulation of capital which low wages made possible in Belgium but not in the Netherlands.

The lesson to be learnt from these comparisons is that there was no pre-determined path from labour-intensive to capital-intensive forms of industrial organization in the eighteenth and nineteenth centuries. Whatever the state of their labour markets, entrepreneurs had to possess the ability as well as the desire to change production methods. In particular, they needed a command of capital which, in the absence of well-developed capital markets, came principally from profits. Here we come to the second of the connections between proto-industry and factory industry stressed by Mendels. Empirical studies, on the whole, confirm the view that the capital for the building and equipping of factories often came from domestic industry. In the English woollen industry for example:

in both Yorkshire and the West of England the majority of the new factory entrepreneurs had had previous connections with the industry, generally through involvement in its domestic organisation. Many of them were able to bring with them financial resources previously gained in the industry. The scale and methods of organisation of domestic manufacture were undoubtedly an influence on the scale and sources of supply of capital for factory development. [49, *39*]

Similarly, a recent study of approximately 150 Arkwright-type cotton mills operating in England in 1787 emphasizes the 'essential continuity of investment' that existed between traditional forms of manufacture and factory production [44, *81*]. The majority of the new mill owners had backgrounds in the textile industry, either as merchants or manufacturers. Nevertheless, there was no inevitability about the flow of capital from one stage of industry to the next. The same study shows that a quarter of the mill owners in the cotton industry in 1787 did *not* emerge from the textile industry but had been bankers, brewers, landowners and the like. This type of investor was exemplified by a clergyman, the Rev. Dr Benson, who was approached by Jedediah Strutt in 1757, on the strength of a prior acquaintance, for a loan to finance a new type of knitting frame. Benson was willing to lend to Strutt, except that his money was tied up in government stock and the proffered rate of return was not high enough to persuade him to switch [4, *28–9*].

Capital therefore sometimes flowed into factory industry from non-industrial sources. It also, on occasions, moved out of cottage industry into other areas of activity, particularly in zones where proto-industry failed to evolve into factory industry. Thus, in East Anglia and the West of England capital shifted into farming, brewing, innkeeping and retail trading. The transition was easy because fixed capital was rarely specific; buildings and sometimes machinery could fairly readily be turned from textile to non-textile uses. Furthermore, liquid capital, which comprised the greater proportion of total capital requirements, could by its very nature be diverted to other uses according to the state of the market for textiles and other goods [see 14]. Fluidity of capital was an essential feature of proto-industry and it is not surprising to find it flowing into whatever channels its owners judged profitable: machine-based industry was just one of several possibilities.

During the transition from the first to the second stages of industrialization there were few hard and fast divisions between capital raising, management and marketing. As the examples just considered suggest, the backgrounds of the investors and the backgrounds of the entrepreneurs were often very similar. Mendels is right, therefore, to emphasize this link between proto-industry and factory industry. His further suggestion, that the machine builders for the new factories came from the world of the old handicraft industry, is more problematical. It is true that traditional mechanical skills were extremely valuable to the first generation of factory owners. For example, in Lancashire one James Greenwood was taken into a cotton-factory partnership in 1784 although 'not having at present any capital to bring into stock' because he has 'a genius well adapted for constructing the machines and other works to be made use of and employed in and about the said intended mill' [quoted 44, 73]. In the textile industry, generally, 'it was from the ranks of the master wheelwrights that many of the early specialist engineers emerged' [86, 80]. Their particular expertise was the calculation of gear ratios and the construction of drive wheels used in milling. However, milling – whether corn, paper or fulling – does not fit into the normal categories of proto-industrial activities for it was centralized and relatively capital-intensive from early times. Furthermore, millwrights were practical, empirical men unlikely, as claimed by Mendels, to be 'in intimate contact with the scientific advances of the time' [64, 244]. The later machine builders in the tradition of Boulton and Watt were more in the scientific mould, but their links with earlier forms of industry were tenuous.

It is unnecessary to labour the point that as the proportion of a country's workforce engaged in industry increased so agricultural productivity needed to be raised. But if improvements in agricultural productivity took place in zones of proto-industry the effect might be to retard rather than to stimulate industrialization since with rising agricultural productivity come rising agricultural earnings which push up the opportunity costs of manufacturing. In England, for example, East Anglia became one of the most advanced agricultural regions of the country during the industrial revolution and its traditional woollen industry declined. In the Low Countries, as Mokyr points out, industrial expansion occurred in Belgium where agricultural productivity was low, but not in the Netherlands where it was high. What was required was that there should be complementary areas of commercializing agriculture and expanding industry, and an intensification of inter-regional and international trade in agricultural and industrial goods. In short, the emergence of modern industry was accompanied by the development of regional specialization.

Proto-industry, then, contained within itself the seeds of further industrial development. But what of those areas that were subject to deindustrialization? Did the seed fall upon stony ground or was it inherently defective? Before attempting to answer these questions a brief checklist of regions of proto-industry that failed to move to the second stage of industrialization is in order. In England two major textile districts, the West of England and East Anglia, failed to develop as centres of factory industry during the eighteenth and early nineteenth centuries. Some lesser centres, including the Weald of Sussex and Kent, had already fallen by the wayside during the seventeenth century. But the most decisive example of industrial failure in the British Isles occurred in Ireland. The woollen industry, which had been moderately prosperous until the 1770s, succumbed to the weight of English competition. More important, by the early decades of the nineteenth century the Ulster linen industry was in difficulties as the result of competition from English cottons. It contracted in the outlying regions and became concentrated near to Belfast. There it became a factory-based industry in the 1820s – a case of a successful transition from proto-industry to modern industry – but at the expense of deindustrialization in north-west and central Ulster [see 21]. On the Continent there were many examples of deindustrialization: 'for instance much of the west of France which had previously developed export-orientated textile industries ... Silesia, Brittany, and Flanders could similarly be ranked on a continuum of relative failure in achieving the transition' [64, 246].

A slightly puzzling feature of the model of proto-industrialization is the way that the high cost of labour has been invoked to explain not only the process of industrialization (the English case), but also the lack of industrialization (the Netherlands case). Conversely, an abundant supply of cheap labour can be used to account for the transition from cottage industry to the factory system (as in Belgium), and also as a reason for the failure of some regions of proto-industry to industrialize. A plentiful supply of cheap labour could be a hindrance to industrialization if it postponed the point at which centralized workshops and labour-saving machinery were introduced into production.

The late starters then had the problems of competing with the products of those regions that had industrialized earlier and some never succeeded in getting back into the race.

There are plenty of examples of traditional forms of industrial organization lingering in districts where labour was cheap. Years ago, for example, Sir John Clapham described in graphic terms how handicraft methods persisted in the textile and hosiery trades in England until the 1840s and 1850s – and even later – sustained by cheap labour recruited from the agricultural districts and from Ireland; and also by the 'weaver's passionate clinging to his loom and his independence; by the consequent automatic turning of weavers' children into weavers' in order to keep up total family income [15, *I*, *552*]. Similarly, the domestic spinning of linen hung on precariously in the most densely populated districts of the west of Ireland until the 1840s, despite the introduction of machine-spinning in the Belfast region two decades earlier which had resulted in a general geographical contraction of the industry [1].

Nevertheless, cheap labour cannot, by itself, be blamed for deindustrialization. In Belgium, as we have noted, it was a positive advantage. Furthermore the persistence of labour-intensive methods of production could reflect, not a perverse attachment to old ways, but an efficient use of factor endowments. France, for example, 'was poorly endowed with coal but had an abundant supply of labour ... The existence of a large reservoir of cheap labour in both urban and rural areas meant that mechanization in industry was considerably less urgent in France than across the channel' [39, *364*]. Eventually, of course, the increased productivity of all factors of production that the new machinery made possible compelled entrepreneurs - if they wished to remain in business - to change their ways. A late start on the road to modern industrialization certainly carried with it the problems of catching up but, as the industrial history of Britain and her competitors in the later nineteenth century shows, the difficulties were not insurmountable. If some regions failed to develop modern forms of industry it was for reasons other than an abundance of labour.

The reasons for deindustrialization in a region can be established only by an examination of the facts of the case. Take Ireland as a case in point. With the exception of a factory-based linen industry in eastern Ulster, and the partial exception of a short-lived cotton industry that grew quickly from the 1780s and declined with almost equal speed from about 1815 to the 1830s, Ireland's traditional industries decayed during the nineteenth century. No totally satisfactory explanation for this decay has yet been supplied, although the problem has often been discussed, most recently by O'Malley and Mokyr [73; 71]. There are, broadly, three inter-related sets of reasons offered. The first is socio-political, stressing the political relationship between Ireland and Britain, especially after the Act of Union in 1801 which exposed Irish industry to competition from technologically superior English industries, unfettered by tariff protection. The limited success of industry in Ulster is attributed to the unique social structure of the province. A weakness of this argument is that it does not explain why Irish industry needed protection in the first place. Thus a second line of reasoning suggests that markets for Irish industrial goods were generally small, so restricting the opportunity for using best-practice methods. The success of the linen industry in Ulster underlines the point since production was largely geared to export markets. Once more, the argument dodges the question why industry, with the exception of linen, was not competitive overseas. We are thus forced into a third set of explanations focusing on supply conditions. Here the crucial problem was that Irish industry lacked capital. But this raises a question. If labour was cheap in Ireland then, on the analogy with Belgium, the accumulation of capital from profit should have been facilitated. Mokyr offers a possible answer by suggesting that low labour costs in Ireland were matched by low productivity [71].

If the Irish example suggests that deindustrialization was a complex process, the case of Silesia seems more straightforward. There, a once prosperous linen trade decayed in the later eighteenth century and factory-based industrialization made only limited progress. The critical influence was political. Linen production had been in the hands of a 'serf-weaver' who paid his landlord a fee for the privilege of weaving as well as other feudal dues and rent. As long as industry flourished these payments, though heavy, were not crippling but in the late eighteenth century Silesian linen producers were suffering from competition from English cottons and Irish linens. At the same time the cost of living was rising. To make matters worse the incorporation of Silesia into Prussia and the Napoleonic wars disrupted markets. Peasant revolts became frequent, but more important for the development of industry, serf-weavers could not afford to invest in their businesses and their landlords were unwilling to do so [53].

But if the decline of Silesia can be attributed to political events how do we account for the failure of some of the old textile regions of England? The gradual decay of the Norfolk worsted industry is perhaps the easiest to explain. From the mid-eighteenth century the region became relatively less important with the rise of Yorkshire but there was no absolute decline until the 1820s. Norfolk may have suffered from Yorkshire competition to some extent, but the two regions tended to specialize in different kinds of cloth. However, the demand for the higher quality Norfolk goods was depressed by changes in fashion, by disruptions of foreign markets caused by war, and – after 1826 following the removal of tariff duties – by competition in England from woollens, worsteds and silks imported from France [see 49]. Norfolk - and East Anglia more widely – might of course have responded to market changes by following the West Riding in manufacturing cheap textiles using the new technologies, but the region lacked coal. It was, however, well endowed to become one of the most efficient agricultural regions of England, a specialism that developed to an increasing extent during the eighteenth and nineteenth centuries.

The decline of the woollen industry in the West of England was also a long drawn out affair spanning over a century from the 1720s to the 1870s. Initially the loss of some foreign markets caused difficulties, but the development of new products and a greater concentration on the home market carried the region successfully through the eighteenth century. There was, in fact, a good deal of investment in machinery and in water- and steam-powered factories. The real decline of the woollen industry in Gloucestershire, Somerset and Wiltshire occurred after the end of the Napoleonic war and even then decay was more relative than absolute until the 1830s when competition from the West Riding factories became severe. Even so, it is not clear why the West of England industry failed to respond sucessfully to Yorkshire competition [61].

The inability of proto-industrialization to explain industrial decline satisfactorily is a major weakness. One feature that all the examples of deindustrialization share in common is that they experienced competition from rival manufacturing regions, causing them to lose markets. However, competition is not in itself an explanation of deindustrialization; we have to look further for reasons why producers in declining regions did not respond dynamically to competition. Political developments, social structures, inappropriate resource endowments: all may go some way to explain why some one-time manufacturing zones suffered industrial failure. But these reasons do not add up to a general explanation of deindustrialization.

Indeed, it may be that there is none, and that the theory of proto-industrialization is causing us to look at the process of industrial development in the wrong light. Many economic writers in eighteenth-century Britain associated economic development with specialization in agriculture or in industry and not with a growth in dual occupations [see 7]. From this perspective the concentration of, say, Ireland in meat or dairy production in the nineteenth century or East Anglia in cereal farming, was not so much deindustrialization as – at the risk of coining yet another polysyllabic noun – a process of 'agriculturization'. The emergence of modern factory industry in some areas from the first stage of proto-industry was necessarily accompanied by a concentration on non-industrial activities in others. The decay of rural industry in regions best suited to agriculture was an inevitable part of the process of economic development.

4 The Social Dimension

The economic rationale of proto-industry was cheap labour. In the previous chapter we identified a number of conditions producing cheap labour in the countryside. The first was where the growth of population had created a supply of labour surplus to the requirements of agriculture. Farms were too small to provide a livelihood for the whole family, there was much underemployment and manufacturers, consequently, were able to recruit labour at very low wages (alternatively, farming families could diversify their activities into part-time industry with little or no loss of agricultural earnings). Second, there was often a good deal of underemployed labour in areas of barren soils. Third, by the eighteenth century there were tillage regions in Europe possessing large numbers of landless labourers who were eager to supplement agricultural earnings by industrial work. The immediate link between proto-industry and social conditions, therefore, was a passive one: where labour was abundant rural industries were likely to develop – as long, of course, as entrepreneurship, capital and markets were also available.

According to the model of proto-industrialization, however, the connexions between rural industry and population growth were more positive than this, with the former actually stimulating the latter. The demographic aspects have been elaborated by Hans Medick [62; 63]. His starting point is the peasant household devoted to agriculture, which was a unit of production, consumption and reproduction. Land was the household's most valued possession for it was the basis of all its wealth. Inheritance customs therefore were directed towards preventing property from passing out of the family's possession. The father determined the choice of his children's marriage partners and the timing of their marriages, which were delayed until the father died or was willing to give up running the farm. The effect of parental control was to keep households simple, composed of parents and unmarried children. Except for the eldest, who inherited the farm, married children were expected to move out of the parental home and set up establishments of their own. In this way the consumption demands on the household were minimized. Even more important, as far as society as a whole was concerned, the mean age at first marriage was kept relatively high, and a substantial minority of people did not marry at all. Thus fertility in the community was low and population grew only slowly.

Members of peasant households, according to Medick, worked together to produce enough food to satisfy their consumption needs. Some output might be sold at the market in order to raise money to pay rents, feudal dues, taxes or tithes, but the primary purpose of family labour was not to produce marketable surpluses but to feed the household. The amount of effort devoted to this task was determined by the size of the family: the more mouths to feed the greater the effort. The cycle of reproduction was important here. A newly married couple with only themselves to feed would do less work than a family with young children. As the older children moved into adolescence there was even more work to be done, although there were then more hands to share it. At the later stages of the life cycle when the family became smaller again, the level of production diminished. If subsistence needs could be met (and rents and taxes paid) by a smaller expenditure of labour – because, for example, a good summer had brought an abundant harvest – then less work was done. In other words, peasants were 'target workers' producing only enough to satisfy conventional wants.

The intrusion of proto-industry altered the operation of peasant households in several ways. Most obviously, manufactured as well as agricultural goods were now the objection of production. More important, though, a proportion of the output of the household was now intended for the market. The family was no longer a closed unit of production and consumption but became enmeshed in the complex network of commerce. It was the influence of these commercial ties on the process of family formation that Medick calls the 'demo-economic system of proto-industrialization' [63, 74].

According to Medick industrial development eroded traditional constraints on early marriage. As they grew into adulthood, children no longer needed to delay marrying until they inherited the farm, for they could now work at least part-time in industry and earn enough money to support themselves. Children became a positive economic asset. Admittedly new-born babies and infants imposed a burden on the household, not least by impairing the mother's ability to work. There was also a high risk that some

40

would die in infancy, in which case the family gained no economic advantage from them. A young mother, though, was likely to give birth to several children, some of whom would survive to an age at which they contributed to the family income. Once the reproductive cycle was in full swing the earnings of the older children offset the costs of the younger ones and the marginal cost of an extra child was small. Proto-industry also enabled married children to remain in the parental home because their labour was now valued. In a large family, a simple division of labour was possible – father weaving, mother spinning, sons assisting at the loom, daughters sewing or embroidering. A large family also ensured that some children would still be at home to support the parents when they became too old or too ill to work.

There was, nevertheless, a perversity in the link between proto-industry and population growth since, in the Medick version of events, a fall in the demand for labour did not lead to a fall in its supply. On the contrary, if the demand for labour declined and wages fell, the family offered more labour, not less, in an attempt to maintain total household income.

Far from promoting prosperity, therefore, proto-industrialization is often seen as bringing poverty to peasant workers and a growing dependence on capitalist merchants. There were several reasons for this unhappy state of affairs. In the first place, as we have observed, the reaction of peasant-manufacturers to falling wages or declining product prices was to work harder in order to maintain total income. Peasants had been forced into manufacturing in the first place because the subsistence they gained from agriculture was inadequate. Nevertheless, their farms supplied them with some of their food and so they were prepared to accept very low prices for their industrial products, or very low wages if they worked for a putting-out merchant. The wages paid to proto-industrial workers were lower than those required by a landless labourer who had to purchase all his food. The tribulations of peasant-manufacturers, though, did not end here. They were propelled even further into poverty by the unstable nature of markets for industrial products. Whenever trade slumped proto-industrial workers were unable to sell their goods or, if they were wage-earners, they were laid off by their employers. Finally, even when they were earning money from industry beyond the needs of immediate consumption, peasant-manufacturers used much of it to acquire additional land for its status value and as an insurance against the uncertainties of the future; but when trade became bad they were left with rents or mortgages which they could not afford. For the peasant, proto-industrialization was the path to immiseration.

In recent years economic and social historians have devoted greater attention to the study of the arcane complexities of family formation than to the more concrete problems of capital formation and have accumulated a good deal of evidence against which the generalizations of proto-industrialization can be tested. We need not spend too much time with Medick's belief that pre-industrial farmers were concerned chiefly with conventional levels of subsistence and were therefore little involved with the market. There is ample evidence to the contrary. The economic history of western Europe from at least the sixteenth century is in large part the story of the growth of commercial farming; and as far as England is concerned Alan MacFarlane has argued powerfully that 'the majority of ordinary people in England from at least the thirteenth century were ... economically "rational", market-orientated and acquisitive, ego-centred in kinship and social life' [60, *163*]. The development of industries in the countryside was far from being the first experience of commercial capitalism in rural areas.

On the other hand, much recent research broadly confirms the view that marriage took place at a relatively late age in western Europe before the industrial revolution. From at least the sixteenth century the mean age at marriage for men seems to have been in the mid to late twenties; and for women it was only a little lower [2; 35]. It also seems clear that general economic expansion – including the development of rural industry – was accompanied by some slight fall in the age at first marriage and by an increase in nuptiality (see below). The position regarding household size is rather more complex. Laslett has argued that in England and western Europe mean household size was under five until the late nineteenth century and that at least 70 per cent of households were two-generational – i.e. they contained only parents and unmarried children [56]. These claims have been strongly challenged but as yet they have not been refuted [see 2]. In some respects, indeed, the small size of households is not surprising if we accept (i) that marriage occurred at a relatively late age, (ii) that mortality – particularly infant mortality – was high, and (iii) that newly married couples set up independent households of their own. In such circumstances, the majority of households were likely to be small and simple.

It is when we come to a consideration of inheritance practices and their influence on family formation and farm size, and of the relationship between them and the development of rural industry, that we find the greatest differences between the generalizations of the model and reality. There was a great variety in the way that land passed from generation to generation, arising, as Joan Thirsk has pointed out, from differences between *law* and *custom*, from the practices followed by property owners and those followed by tenants, and from an abundance of land in some regions and a scarcity in others. There were also, to complicate matters further, changes in law and custom over time [88]. To make matters even more involved, the existence of a vigorous market in land could cut across the effects of any inheritance customs. In these circumstances generalizations are likely to be misleading. England, for example, is usually regarded as a country where primogeniture (i.e. the bequeathing of property to the first-born child, or more usually to the first-born son) was general, and France as a region of partible inheritance (i.e. the bequeathing of property to all the children or, more commonly, to the sons). In reality, a variety of conditions existed in all countries.

The practical consequences of primogeniture and partible inheritance might be quite similar. Even when the former was practised it was unusual for no provision at all to be made for younger sons or for daughters, and so as property was transmitted from generation to generation there was a slight tendency for it to become divided. On the other hand, partible inheritance by its very nature produced a subdivision of property, but unless population was growing rapidly the fragmentation was unlikely to be excessive [9].

The relevance of this discussion for proto-industrialization is that it is impossible to predict that any one type of inheritance practice will be associated with purely agrarian economies and a different type with rural-industrial economies. Wherever land was scarce and farms were small the community might well move from a system of partible inheritance to one of primogeniture in order to prevent further subdivision. The growth of rural industry might make the need less pressing by providing an income to supplement that derived from the land. To this extent, therefore, proto-industry might be associated with partible inheritance. However, the development of intensive tillage cultivation in the place of extensive pastoral farming or the introduction of new high-yielding crops –

43

the potato, for example – could have the same effect. Conversely, primogeniture, by preventing the subdivision of farms, tended to create a class of landless labourers, and, as we have seen in the case of the Pays de Caux, such people were sometimes recruited into rural industry.

Just as we cannot assume that a particular pattern of inheritance was associated with rural industry, so we cannot assume that agrarian households were small and simple and proto-industrial households were large and complex. Indeed, the connexion might be the other way round. In agrarian societies shortages of land, patriarchal control of marriage, and impartible inheritance might produce households composed of parents, the eldest married son and his wife, and adult unmarried siblings unable to marry or acquire a farm of their own (the so-called 'stem' family); whereas rural industry with its opportunities for additional earning might enable the children to marry at an early age and set up a home independently of their parents.

Some specific examples will illustrate the complexities of the connexions between economic conditions and demographic structures. The Leicestershire village of Shepshed was a community composed of freehold cultivators; their holdings were small and their incomes low. From the late seventeenth century the villagers became increasingly involved with framework knitting organized by London-based capitalists; by the end of the eighteenth century the village had become one of the most industrialized in the county. The demographic effects seem quite clear. During the course of the eighteenth century the mean age at first marriage for both men and women fell by about five years, from the high to the low twenties. The reduction in marriage ages had a direct effect on marital fertility which rose significantly through the century. The lowering of the age at marriage and the increase in fertility further reinforced the rate of population growth by changing the age structure of the population and progressively enlarging the size of the child-bearing age cohort.

These developments may be contrasted with the demographic history of the nearby but purely agricultural village of Bottesford. This was a landlord-dominated community of tenant farmers which from the later seventeenth century was increasingly turning away from growing corn to fattening and grazing. Employment opportunities in agriculture contracted, there was no rural industry to provide alternative employment, and during the eighteenth century the age at first marriage rose, fertility fell and the rate of population growth declined. Shepshed and Bottesford represent two very different demographic histories in the eighteenth century [58].

In Ireland, the influence of linen spinning and weaving on demographic behaviour has been investigated by Almquist, making use of information contained in the 1841 census. He found that spinners and weavers were most numerous in regions with the greatest population densities, that nuptiality was high and marriage ages were low among spinners and weavers; and that areas containing relatively large numbers of spinners were also areas with relatively high proportions of children in the population. He concluded that the opportunity for employment in textiles increased female nuptiality, but so too did the availability of waste land. Although Almquist's data relate to a period when many parts of Ireland were already deindustrializing, they give support to the view that rural industry and rapid population growth were positively correlated [1].

Studies of regions in continental Europe point in the same direction. In eighteenth-century Flanders, for example, farms in the maritime zone (the Polders) were large and undivided and devoted to commercial agriculture. In the inland districts, however, the land had been divided into many tiny family farms whose occupants were engaged in labour-intensive agriculture and in linen manufacture:

> The population of the Flemish interior grew twice as fast as the population of the Polders ... In the interior the annual number of marriages increased with the prosperity of the linen industry while in the Polders it did not. On the other hand, in the Polders, marriages increased with the prosperity of the commercial agriculture. In both areas, therefore, marriages were noticeably responsive to changes in the market economy. [9, *218*]

In neither area, incidentally, did the system of inheritance have much effect on the size of farms.

A final example is provided by the Swiss canton of Zurich. By the end of the eighteenth century about one-third of the population was employed in various branches of the textile industry. This semi-industrial population, however, was concentrated in the mountainous region of the canton and not in the lowland zone which was purely agrarian. This latter region was composed of closed village communities where farming practices, land use, house building and settlement were strictly regulated. Rural industry had little opportunity to develop. The population grew only slowly and population surpluses emigrated. Some of them moved to the highland zone which at the beginning of the eighteenth century was sparsely populated. Soils were poor and, in contrast to the lowland region, there were few community controls on economic activities, building and settlement. The settler population combined farming and manufacturing, working with materials put out to them by capitalist-merchants. Marriages were numerous and were contracted at an early age, and the population of the highland zone grew rapidly [11].

It seems reasonably clear from these examples that rural industry encouraged the growth of population by lowering the mean age at first marriage, thereby contributing to an increase in fertility – though it should be noted that much of the discussion is based on the marriage behaviour of males, whereas it is the age of females that is important. Proto-industry could also contribute to an increase in population by reducing mortality. This could happen if the extra earnings provided by manufacturing enabled the family to live at a higher standard than was provided by farming alone. We will return to a consideration of living standards in proto-industrial families later. For the moment, though, it should be noted that recent demographic studies stress the fertility rather than the mortality link.

We must not assume that proto-industry was the only cause of the acceleration of population growth during the eighteenth and early nineteenth centuries. Wrigley and Schofield have shown that the increase in England's population from the 1730s was associated with a general economic expansion leading to a rise in nuptiality (but not to any dramatic decline in marriage ages) [96]. At a more local level, Levine demonstrates that between 1775 and 1851 the population of the agricultural village of Terling in Essex grew even faster than the population of the framework-knitting village of Shepshed. Terling was affected, not by industrial expansion but by the growth of commercial agriculture. Levine concluded that 'undermining a traditional economy and replacing it with one where capitalist agriculture or proto-industry held sway had identifiable demographic implications' [58, *147*]. Ireland offers an even more striking case of rapid population growth resting on agricultural rather than on industrial expansion.

In Medick's demographic model population grows as industry expands but growth does not cease when industry goes into decline. The reality was more complex. Levine's study of Shepshed shows that in times of depression the mean age at marriage of men rose although this was not the case with women. Since of course it was the age at which women married that was crucial to fertility a change in the behaviour of men had little effect on population growth. However, there was another strategy open to married couples when times were bad: they could resort to contraception (using *coitus interruptus*) to restrict the size of their families. Family limitation was apparently adopted by framework knitters in Leicestershire during the chronically depressed years after 1825 [58].

Yet another reaction to a fall in the demand for labour was emigration. This process has been studied, for example, in Ulster by Collins. As the Ulster linen industry suffered competition from the English cotton industry, and also from coarse machine-spun English linen yarns, depression hit the northern and western counties, and whole families migrated. Later, in the 1840s, the industry contracted also in north-central Ireland with a consequential outflow of people from that part of the province. Before the Famine emigration from Ireland was greatest from those regions most affected by the decay of the linen industry [21]. Finally, of course, the most basic demographic consequence of deteriorating conditions was a rise in infant mortality, such as occurred in Shepshed in the second quarter of the nineteenth century.

Lying behind these discussions of the response of population to industrialization is an assumption in much of the literature that families were economically rational in their demographic behaviour. That is to say, peasants and proto-industrial workers are believed to have made their decisions about marrying according to whether land or employment were available. This assumed rationality also extends to couples calculating the numbers of children they could afford, which depended on the amount of work that was available. As Collins puts it, 'patterns of family formation are affected by the differential availability of employment for family members ...' [21, *133*]. Farmer-weavers needed the labour of their sons and so endeavoured to keep them at home when they reached maturity. They also needed their wives and daughters to perform those tasks traditionally regarded as female occupations. Households lacking the appropriate age and sex mix were obliged to hire journeymen and apprentices, or perhaps to buy in materials they could not produce themselves. It was quite common in Ulster, for example, for linen weavers to purchase yarn spun by widows and unmarried women. Households composed of widows and unmarried daughters earning their living by spinning were common, and they were often very small – thus running counter to the predictions of proto-industrialization. They were economically viable because of the unbalanced demographic structure of some of the weaving households [16].

The problem with making assumptions about the attitudes of peasant workers is that they can rarely be proved. Contemporary observers sometimes commented on attitudes, or they may be deduced by social historians from sources which, as Louise Tilly puts it, 'tell *about* people rather than ... [were] created *by* people' [90, *137*]. It was not in the nature of peasant-manufacturers to make explicit their motives on such intimate matters as marriage and procreation. Tilly's solution to the absence of personal records is to adopt the 'concept of family strategies' which 'tries to uncover the principles which lead to observable regularities or patterns of behaviour among households'. In other words. by studying groups of families and observing regularities in their behaviour she believes it is possible to make statements about motives. Thus an investigation of large numbers of proto-industrial workers in Zurich has led Braun to argue that:

> putting-out industry gave girls and boys the material prerequisites for marriage, and this possibility did away with any hesitation or fears that the young might have about knowing and getting to love each other. With no material considerations to stand in the way, one could yield to the attractions of the other sex. [11, *315*]

It is difficult to see that Braun's judgement is any less an assumption of motives for the behaviour of an inarticulate mass of individuals by being based on a large sample of households than it would have been for resting on the study of only a few. The 'family strategy' concept does not really get over the problem of explaining as opposed to describing behaviour.

We come, finally, to an assessment of the belief contained in much of the literature of proto-industrialization that rural industry caused the immiseration of peasant manufacturers. If by immiseration is meant lower earnings than could be obtained in alternative employments, then the proposition is not firmly established either logically or empirically. It may be true that the earnings of workers in cottage industry were very low, but even on the assumptions of the model they were higher than could be earned from agriculture alone [see 70]. Whether earnings of proto-industrial workers were lower than those accruing to purely industrial workers with no land to fall back on is a moot point. Rural linen workers in late eighteenth-century Flanders earned slightly less than other unskilled rural workers and considerably less than urban craftsmen, but the alternative before them was underemployment and totally inadequate agricultural earnings [65]. In England, to take another example, framework knitters in Shepshed in the 1830s and 1840s were certainly impoverished, they lived in overcrowded conditions and their mortality was higher than that of their agricultural neighbours [58]. But this was at the end of three-quarters of a century of rapid population growth when the industry was suffering from the competition of technologically superior processes; the picture at an earlier stage may have been different.

Empirical investigations elsewhere suggest that rural industry actually raised levels of living. In the English metal-working districts of the West Midlands and South Yorkshire in the seventeenth and eighteenth centuries, the levels of comfort enjoyed by metal craftsmen were as high or higher than those of the neighbouring farmers and labourers [38; 82]. In Ulster an observer noted in 1812 that in linen households, because the weaver 'supplies work to everyone under his roof, he is enabled by their earnings to consume oatmeal instead of potatoes and to allow his wife and children to wear cotton or linen gowns' [quoted 21, *135*]; almost half a century earlier Arthur Young and others had remarked on a similar relative prosperity among linen workers. Admittedly proto-industrial workers often were extremely poor. As Mendels points out, poverty and unemployment co-existed with proto-industrialization [65]; but this is not the same as saying that proto-industry created more poverty than existed in purely agrarian societies.

It seems, however, that when writers such as Medick refer to immiseration they have in mind, not so much earnings or living conditions, as the changing relationship between peasant-manufac-turers and the merchants who linked them to the market. It is undeniable that proto-industrialization accelerated, although it did not initiate, the growth of a wage-earning class dependent on capitalist employers for their livelihoods. This loss of independence undermined what Medick and others have called the 'plebeian culture' of the proto-industrial family economy: the right to work when it chose; to engage in 'traditional leisure time rituals'; to be part of a local village community; to enjoy traditional patterns of consumption. From this perspective even the extra consumption that industrial wages made possible is evidence of worsening living and working conditions: 'coffee, tea, and alcohol became necessary stimulants as the conditions of production deteriorated and work became more degrading' [63, 69].

As with discussions of the attitudes of proto-industrial workers towards marriage and children, it is very difficult to show that the wage nexus was, in fact, regarded by the workers themselves in the dismal manner that some historians assume. If the yoke of industrial capitalism did indeed weigh so heavily on the once-independent peasant, then it must be remembered that it burdened him also with the additional purchasing power with which to buy an ever widening range of consumption goods. It also conferred on him the opportunity of marrying early and to a wife of his own choosing.

5 Conclusion: The Model Assessed

We stated in the introduction that models in history are intended, first, to provide a generalized description of events that occurred, or seem to have occurred, with some regularity in the past; and, second, to offer explanations of how events changed over time. Proto-industrialization is concerned with the widespread presence of industries in the European countryside in the century or so before the industrial revolution and the way in which these cottage industries evolved into modern factory industrialization. There is also a third and more ambitious purpose of models: to discover in the past policy prescriptions for the present and future. How far does the particular model under discussion meet these objectives?

The proto-industrialization thesis has two parts: the economic and the social. As far as the former is concerned, proto-industry was a phase of industrial development found in many parts of Europe between the later seventeenth century and the industrial revolution in which manufacturing was carried out in rural cottages by men, women and children who divided their time between agriculture and industry. The goods they produced were destined, not for local consumption, but for world-wide markets. Peasant-manufacturers lived in regions where, for a variety of reasons, agricultural incomes were low and cultivators therefore had a strong incentive to turn to manufacturing to supplement them. The link between peasant-producers and the wider world was provided by merchants who visited the market towns in the regions of cottage industry to buy manufactured goods. Towns were not primarily centres of industrial production but places where proto-industrial workers disposed of their goods, obtained supplies of raw materials and bought such food as they were unable to grow themselves. This food came from areas of commercial agriculture where farmers devoted themselves to growing crops for sale and did not engage in manufacturing to any great extent.

This description has the merit of capturing many features of the industrial life of western Europe before the industrial revolution. It has the additional merit of being applicable also to non-European societies and so facilitating comparisons across regions and

51

continents [see 75]. But the concept has many limitations. The most obvious is chronology. Taking the manufacture of woollen textiles as an example of what is now fashionable to call proto-industry, the production of goods for distant markets by workers who combined farming with spinning and weaving had been a characteristic feature of European economic life long before the seventeenth century. Furthermore, there had been a considerable growth of rural textile production during the later middle ages in England, the Netherlands and elsewhere, for the very reasons offered by proponents of proto-industrialization to explain the growth of rural industry in the late seventeenth and eighteenth centuries: i.e. growing competition in international markets which induced manufacturers to seek ways of reducing costs by employing country labour [see 20; 69; 92]. In the light of these earlier developments it is difficult to see why the years after 1650 should be picked out as the critical phase of proto-industrialization. The reason must be that in western Europe the period from the mid-seventeenth century culminated with the industrial revolution; in the language of the model, proto-industrialization was followed by a second phase of factory industrialization. An assumption has been made that the chronological sequence of years was matched by a logical progression from one form of industrial organization to another. Closer attention to the 'proto-industries' of the later middle ages, however, would demonstrate the fallacy of such an assumption.

Even if the ignoring of the earlier presence of rural industries and the concentrating on their later manifestations could be justified, this would not dispose of the problem of dating. As a phase in industrial development proto-industrialization is as untidy at its ending as at its beginning. There is no need to labour the point that the timing of the onset of modern industrialization is extremely difficult to determine. As late as 1851 the majority of people employed in Britain – the most advanced of the industrial nations – still worked in the unmechanized sectors. Cottage industry did not disappear with the development of factories, even in those branches of production most affected by the innovation of new machinery.

A central feature of the concept of proto-industrialization is the emphasis it places on the combination of agricultural and industrial occupations. However, any student even superficially acquainted with the nature of pre-industrialized economies will know that there was a low level of occupational specialization throughout society, reflecting the limited opportunities provided by the market. Proto-industrialization, notwithstanding, associates dual occupations with particular types of agrarian systems; it also postulates that they actually became more common as market opportunities opened up for peasant-manufacturers. Such an interpretation would have puzzled Adam Smith, who argued that widening markets created greater opportunities for occupational specialization. So it is worth emphasizing that as the demand for industrial products increased during the eighteenth century, the amount of time that peasant-manufacturers devoted to farming seems to have diminished. In places as far apart as the linen-producing areas of County Armagh in Ireland, and the framework-knitting villages of Leicestershire in England, industry had almost displaced agriculture as a source of income by the end of the eighteenth century.

We also need to remember that the geography of proto-industry was not always of the kind suggested by the model. Once again using the textile industries as an illustration, there were indeed many areas of Europe where the manufacture of textiles was combined with the cultivation of poor soils and tiny farms. But there were also rural industrial zones that did not fit into this pattern. In eighteenth-century Ulster the finest linen manufacturing was undertaken in the northern part of County Armagh which was a fertile region capable of producing food surpluses. In eighteenth-century Normandy the manufacture of cotton textiles, using cottage labour, developed in a tillage zone. In England, both the Suffolk and the Wiltshire woollen industries were found in association with pastoral farming, a connexion that the model explains by arguing that caring for animals left farmers time to spare for spinning and weaving. Yet, as pastoral farming developed in the Leicestershire village of Bottesford during the eighteenth century, the manufacture of hosiery did *not* become important in the parish, although it did so in villages nearby [58]. The conclusion to be drawn is that cheap rural labour, attractive to industrial producers and merchants, could develop in a variety of agrarian systems which cannot be neatly embraced in a generalized model.

Before leaving the geography of proto-industry we should recall that the model stresses the importance of towns as marketing centres and neglects their importance as centres of manufacture. This arises from the fact that the archetypal proto-industrial worker is seen as one who combined farming with manufacturing and almost by definition such people were not common in towns.

Nevertheless, industry organized on a domestic or putting-out basis was an important part of the economies of many towns in England and western Europe. Many urban workers followed more than one occupation for the same reason as their rural counterparts: to maximize total income. From the point of view of the employer or the merchant it did not matter a jot whether labourers lived in towns or in the countryside as long as their cost was cheap. For high-quality products, indeed, towns were better locations, for skills were likely to be available and employers could more readily supervise manufacturing processes.

We now come to what is perhaps the most serious weakness of proto-industrialization as a description of 'industrialization before industrialization': it is very restricted in the range of occupations that it encompasses. Practically all the examples are drawn from the woollen, linen and cotton industries. There are glancing references to other activies such as the manufacture of metal or leather goods, but little else. Also excluded are the great multitude of manufacturing occupations found in pre-industrial towns and villages, such as woodworking, thatching, glazing, building, tailoring, dressmaking, brewing, shoemaking, in fact all those activities catering for local demands for essential consumer goods but not geared to distant and overseas markets. Neither are the more capital-intensive enterprises such as iron-smelting, mining, milling and paper-making embraced by the notion of proto-indus-trialization. The reason for their neglect, of course, is that such forms of manufacturing do not fit into the dynamic aspects of the model.

How good, in fact, is proto-industrialization in explaining the development of modern factory-based industry? If the industrial revolution were merely a matter of the textile industries, the model might be regarded as a useful though incomplete explanation of how cottage workshops came to be replaced by centralized factories. It does not capture all the complexities of reality – such as the simultaneous existence of dispersed cottage workers, centralized workshops using hand-operated machines, and factories operated by water or steam power – but then models are always simplified versions of the truth. However, modern industrialization compris-ed much more than the textile industries, although, admittedly, these were central to the early stages of industrialization in Europe; an explanation of industrialization that has almost nothing to say about, for example, the metal-smelting and mining industries is clearly incomplete. These industries did not, in their early development, display the characteristics of the first stage of industrialization as identified by the model and they are therefore ignored. This brings us back to an earlier criticism, that as a description of the first or 'proto' stage of industry the model is concerned only with those branches of manufacture that evolved in a particular way.

Even as an explanation of the growth of the textile and similarly organized industries, the internal dynamics of the model lack precision. Thus, it is argued that rising labour costs eventually made rural workshops uneconomic and so promoted the growth of modern factory industrialization. But it is also argued that increased labour costs inhibited the development of the second stage of industry by cutting into profits and therefore preventing the necessary accumulation of capital. This uncertainty as to the effects of shifting factor costs is related to a still greater difficulty. According to the model, proto-industry might be followed either by modern industrialization or by deindustrialization. It is not possible to discover from general principles why a particular course of development occurred. Particular case-studies indicate that political and social structures existing within a region were important in determining whether or not there would be further industrial development, but the operation of these influences has to be established by empirical research.

What of the social aspects of proto-industrialization? According to the model marriages were contracted at a younger age in areas of rural industry than elsewhere, families were larger, and households more complex. The model also suggests that the motivation for marriage was different among peasant-manufacturers, with young couples marrying because of romantic attachments and not as a business arrangement organized by their parents. A good deal of empirical evidence has been assembled to demonstrate that the age at first marriage was indeed relatively low among peasant-manufacturing households; but as the case of Ireland shows, other influences, such as easy access to land or cheap food, could also facilitate young marriages in farming communities. The evidence concerning the size and structure of households reveals a more complicated picture. A family's need for cheap labour provided an incentive to keep children at home and to accommodate other relatives; on the other hand the income derived from rural industry made it possible for young men and women to set up households of their own, thus creating smaller family units. Similarly, widows living by themselves or with adolescent children could survive as

55

small independent households by spinning yarn, embroidering or carrying out other ancillary tasks in the textile industry [see 16]. As to the reasons why marriages were entered into by cottage workers, we remarked in Chapter 4 that historians are largely guessing at motives from behaviour, the individuals themselves being almost totally silent on the matter.

Another social feature of proto-industrialization is the assertion that as peasant households became enmeshed in the commercial production of industrial goods individuals suffered a decline in their social and economic condition, with once independent producers being turned into wage-earners and suffering 'immiseration'. We noted, though, in Chapter 2 that the model does not provide convincing reasons why cottage workers sometimes were self-employed producers and at other times were wage-earners. Nor is it clear from the model why wage-earning should have become more prevalent as time went by. On the matter of immiseration, both the logic of the model and empirical studies suggest that proto-industrial workers were wealthier than they would have been in the absence of industry; and the increased purchasing power they enjoyed permitted them to buy commodities which, even if they were bad for their health and morals, were the goods that they desired.

The model is probably most useful in drawing attention to the changes that could take place in peasant households as industrialization got under way, although, as we have noted, those changes could be complex. It is the relationship between early industrialization and peasant labour that has led development economists to look to the past and has persuaded some historians that their researches are relevant to the problems of the developing world. According to historians who have formulated the model, industry expanded in western Europe in the century and a half before the industrial revolution on the basis of cheap labour in the countryside. For countries in the underdeveloped world today possessing abundant supplies of cheap labour the European experience seems, superficially, to point to a possible path of development.

However, any testing of the model of proto-industrialization against the realities of the European past reveals its limitations. It is doubtful, therefore, whether the development economist will really gain much guidance for the future from the European experience, except for the important but frequently forgotten lesson that economic and social changes are always very complex events. As for the historian, he will find the concept of proto-industrialization more helpful in prompting him to look afresh at the process of industrial development than in providing him with explanations of his findings.

Bibliography

As an introduction to the subject for English-speaking readers, this bibliography concentrates on works in English. References to publications in other languages, chiefly French and German, may be found in [28], [54] and [79]. Recent issues of journals such as *Annales, Journal of European Economic History, Journal of Family History* and *Social History* contain much relevant material. Because proto-industrialization is part of a long debate in history on the origins of modern industrial society I have included works which are not part of the proto-industrial canon, and also those that are critical of it. Broadly speaking, anything published before 1970 is uncoloured by the concept, and not everything published since is in agreement wth it.

[1] E.L. Almquist, 'Pre-Famine Ireland and the Theory of European Proto-industrialization: the Evidence from the 1841 Census', *Journal of Economic History*, XXXIX (1979). Uses the 1841 census to test the relationship between population density and rural industry.

[2] M. Anderson, *Approaches to the History of the Western Family 1500–1914* (1980). A valuable introduction to the subject.

[3] T.S. Ashton, *The Industrial Revolution, 1760–1830* (1948). Remains the best short introduction to the subject by far.

[4] T.S. Ashton, *An Economic History of England: the 18th Century* (1955). Chapter VII is an excellent analysis of the eighteenth-century labour market and the whole book is a perceptive account of economic development on the eve of the industrial revolution.

[5] T.S. Ashton, *Economic Fluctuations in England, 1700–1800* (1959). Should be read together with [4].

[6] M. Barkhausen, 'Government Control and Free Enterprise in Western Germany and the Low Countries in the Eighteenth Century', in P. Earle (ed.), *Essays in European Economic History, 1500–1800* (1974). A wide-ranging and detailed regional study. Should be read together with [53].

[7] M. Berg, 'Political Economy and the Principles of

Manufacture 1700–1800', in [8]. A survey of contemporary perceptions of industrialization.

[8] M. Berg, P. Hudson and M. Sonenscher, *Manufacture in Town and Country before the Factory* (1983). Seven essays critical of proto-industrialization.

[9] L.K. Berkner and F.F. Mendels, 'Inheritance Systems, Family Structure, and Demographic Patterns in Western Europe, 1700–1900', in C. Tilly (ed.), *Historical Studies of Changing Fertility* (1978). A study of the relationship between access to land, family formation and economic activity.

[10] R. Braun, 'The Impact of Cottage Industry on an Agricultural Population', in D.S. Landes (ed.), *The Rise of Capitalism* (1966). Studies the effect of rural industry on family formation in Switzerland. Extract from a longer study published in German.

[11] R. Braun, 'Early Industrialization and Demographic Change in the Canton of Zurich', in C. Tilly (ed.), *Historical Studies of Changing Fertility* (1978). A much elaborated and fully documented statement of the argument in [10].

[12] R. Brenner, 'Agrarian Class Structure and Economic Development in Pre-industrial Europe', *Past & Present*, 70 (1976). A restatement of the Marxist view of long-run economic development. Has provoked a lively debate. See *Past & Present*, 78 (1978), 79 (1978), 80 (1978) and 85 (1979).

[13] J.D. Chambers, *Nottinghamshire in the Eighteenth Century* (1932). A classic regional study.

[14] S.D. Chapman, 'Industrial Capital before the Industrial Revolution: An Analysis of the Assets of a Thousand Textile Entrepreneurs c. 1730–50', in [36]. A useful empirical study. See also [44].

[15] J.H. Clapham, *An Economic History of Modern Britain:* I *The Early Railway Age, 1820–1850* (1926); II *Free Trade and Steel, 1850–1886* (1932); III *Machines and National Rivalries, 1887–1914, with an Epilogue, 1914–1929* (1938). A masterly account of industrialization in Britain emphasizing the gradual nature of the process.

[16] L.A. Clarkson and B. Collins, 'Proto-industrialization in an Irish Town: Lisburn, 1821', in [28]. A study of an urban linen and cotton industry in domestic workshops.

[17] D.C. Coleman, 'Industrial Growth and Industrial Revolutions', *Economica* (1956); reprinted in E.M.

Carus-Wilson (ed.), *Essays in Economic History*, III (1962). A powerful plea for not calling every industrial spurt before the late eighteenth century a revolution.

[18] D.C. Coleman, 'An Innovation and its Diffusion: the "New Draperies"', *Economic History Review*, 2nd ser., XXII (1969). Analyses the way in which peasant manufacture becomes linked to international markets.

[19] D.C. Coleman, *Industry in Tudor and Stuart England* (1975). A succinct survey of industry in pre-industrialized England.

[20] D.C. Coleman, 'Proto-industrialization: A Concept Too Many', *Economic History Review*, 2nd ser., XXXVI (1983). A highly sceptical critique of the concept. Essential reading.

[21] B. Collins, 'Proto-industrialization and Pre-famine Emigration', *Social History*, 7(1982). A study of decline in the Ulster linen industry in the early nineteenth century and its effects on the family economy.

[22] P. Corfield, 'A provincial Capital in the late Seventeenth Century: the Case of Norwich', in P. Clark and P. Slack (eds), *Crisis and Order in English Towns, 1500–1700* (1972). Demonstrates the importance of textile manufacture to the economy of an English city.

[23] W.H.B. Court, *The Rise of the Midland Industries, 1600–1838* (1938). A classic study of early industrialization, concentrating on mining and metallurgy.

[24] W.H. Crawford, 'The Origins of the Linen Industry in North Armagh and the Lagan Valley', *Ulster Folklife*, 17 (1971). With [25] an important qualification of the arguments contained in [32].

[25] W.H. Crawford, 'Economy and Society in South Ulster in the Eighteenth Century', *Clogher Record* (1975).

[26] W. Cunningham, *The Growth of English Industry and Commerce* (1882). The first general textbook on English economic history containing many examples of rural industries before the eighteenth century. Strongly influenced by the stage theories of economic development discussed in [45].

[27] J. De Vries, *The Economy of Europe in an Age of Crisis 1600–1750* (1976). A general textbook incorporating the theory of proto-industrialization into its analysis.

[28] P. Deyon and F.F. Mendels (eds), *La Protoindustrialisation: Théorie et Réalité*, 2 vols (1982). Proceedings of the Eighth

International Conference on Economic History held in Budapest containing forty-eight essays in three languages and dealing with three continents. At present in mimeographed form, but publication is threatened.

[29] M. Dobb, *Studies in the Development of Capitalism* (1946). An important Marxist statement.

[30] M.W. Flinn, *Origins of the Industrial Revolution* (1966). A useful survey of interpretations of industrialization before the proto-industrialization literature appeared.

[31] E.W. Gilboy, *Wages in Eighteenth Century England* (1934). An old but still useful empirical study.

[32] C. Gill, *The Rise of the Irish Linen Industry* (1925). Still the standard work, but needs to be read in conjunction with [24] and [25].

[33] J. Goody, J. Thirsk and E.P. Thompson, *Family and Inheritance: Rural Society in Western Europe 1200–1800* (1976). A useful collection of essays.

[34] G.L. Gullickson, 'Agriculture and Cottage Industry: Redefining the Causes of Proto-industrialization', *Journal of Economic History*, XLIII (1983). Challenges the view that proto-industry was associated only with subsistence or pastoral agriculture. Based on a study of the Pays de Caux in Normandy.

[35] J. Hajnal, 'European Marriage Patterns in Perspective', in D.V. Glass and D.E.C. Eversley (eds), *Population in History: Essays in Historical Demography* (1965). An important essay arguing for a relatively late age of marriage in western Europe.

[36] N.B. Harte and K.G. Ponting (eds), *Textile History and Economic History: Essays in Honour of Miss Julia de Lacy Mann* (1973). Fifteen essays on aspects of the English textile industry.

[37] H. Heaton, *The Yorkshire Woollen and Worsted Industries from Earliest Times up to the Industrial Revolution* (1920). An old but still important study.

[38] D. Hey, *The Rural Metalworkers of the Sheffield Region: A Study of Rural Industry before the Industrial Revolution* (1972). A useful empirical study.

[39] C. Heywood, 'The Role of the Peasantry in French Industrialization, 1815–80', *Economic History Review*, XXXIV (1981). Critical of the view that the structure of agrarian society inhibited industrialization in France.

61

[40] R.H. Hilton *et al.*, *The Transition from Feudalism to Capitalism* (1978). Contributions to the Marxist debate on industrialization.

[41] R.H. Hilton, 'Capitalism: What's in a Name?', in [40].

[42] E.J. Hobswawm, 'The Crisis of the Seventeenth Century', *Past & Present*, 5 and 6 (1954); reprinted in T. Aston (ed.), *Crisis in Europe, 1560–1660* (1965). Argues that seventeenth-century Europe suffered an economic 'crisis' that was eventually overcome by 'the triumph of capitalism'.

[43] E.J. Hobsbawm, 'From Feudalism to Capitalism', in [40].

[44] K. Honeyman, *Origins of Enterprise: Business Leadership in the Industrial Revolution* (1982). A study of entrepreneurship in lead mining, cotton spinning and lace manufacture. See also [14].

[45] B.F. Hoselitz, 'Theories of Stages of Economic Growth', in B.F. Hoselitz (ed.), *Theories of Economic Growth* (1960). A review of the work of the German school of historical economists.

[46] R. Houston and K. Snell, 'Proto-industrialization? Cottage Industry, Social Change, and Industrial Revolution', *Historical Journal*, 27 (1984). An extended review of [54]. Highly critical, with excellent references.

[47] P. Hudson, 'Proto-industrialization: the Case of the West Riding Wool Textile Industry in the 18th and early 19th Centuries', *History Workshop Journal*, 12 (1981). An important critical article. See also her essay in [8].

[48] S. Hymer and S. Resnick, 'A Model of an Agrarian Economy with Nonagricultural Activities', *American Economic Review*, 59 (1969). A theoretical discussion of rural industry. See also [59].

[49] D.T. Jenkins and K.G. Ponting, *The British Wool Textile Industry 1770–1914* (1982). A very useful survey.

[50] E.L. Jones, 'Agricultural Origins of Industry', *Past & Present*, 40 (1968); reprinted in E.L. Jones, *Agriculture and the Industrial Revolution* (1974). Argues that rural industry developed in Europe from the later seventeenth century in farming regions not well suited to cereal production.

[51] L. Jorberg (ed.), 'Proto-industrialization in Scandinavia', *Scandinavian Economic History Review*, XXX (1982). Issue devoted to a discussion of the concept as applied to the textile, wood-working and metal-working industries in Denmark, Finland, Norway and Sweden. Highly sceptical.

[52] H. Kellenbenz, 'Rural Industries in the West from the End of the Middle Ages to the Eighteenth Century', in P. Earle (ed.), *Essays in European Economic History, 1500–1800* (1974). A comprehensive regional survey.

[53] H. Kisch, 'The Textile Industries in Silesia and the Rhineland: A Comparative Study in Industrialization', *Journal of Economic History*, XIX (1959); reprinted in [54]. An important empirical study pre-dating the proto-industrial literature.

[54] P. Kriedte, H. Medick and J. Schlumbohm, *Industrialization before Industrialization* (1981). First published in German in 1979. Translation is only partly to blame for the proliferation of polysyllabic nouns and almost endless sentences. Eight important essays on all aspects of proto-industrialization. Excellent bibliography.

[55] P. Kriedte, 'Proto-industrialization between Industrialization and De-industrialization', in [54].

[56] P. Laslett and R. Wall (eds), *Household and Family in Past Time* (1972). A pioneering collection of essays on family size and structure, sometimes displaying premature generalization. See also [94].

[57] R.D. Lee and R.S. Schofield, 'British Population in the Eighteenth Century', in R. Floud and D. McCloskey (eds), *The History of Britain since 1700*, I (1981). Succinct survey of eighteenth-century demography. See also [96].

[58] D. Levine, *Family Formation in an Age of Nascent Capitalism* (1977). Probably the most detailed local study in England of the relationship between family formation and early industrialization.

[59] W.A. Lewis, 'Economic Development with Unlimited Supplies of Labour', in A.N. Agarwala and S.P. Singh (eds), *The Economics of Underdevelopment* (1958). With [48] supplies much of the theoretical underpinning for the model of proto-industrialization.

[60] A. Macfarlane, *The Origins of English Individualism: The Family, Property and Social Transition* (1978). Iconoclastic and stimulating. Should be contrasted with [62] and [63].

[61] J. de L. Mann, *The Cloth Industry in the West of England from 1640 to 1880* (1971). A study of the final era of a once-important textile region.

[62] H. Medick, 'The Proto-industrial Family Economy: The Structural Function of Household and Family during the

Transition from Peasant to Industrial Capitalism', *Social History*, I (1976); reprinted, with elaborations, in [54]. The seminal statement on the relationship between industrialization and family formation.

[63] H. Medick, 'The Structures and Function of Population development under the Proto-industrial System', in [54]. A further elaboration of the argument in [62].

[64] F.F. Mendels, 'Proto-industrialization: The First Phase of the Industrialization Process', *Journal of Economic History*, XXXII (1972). The seminal article on the subject.

[65] F.F. Mendels, 'Agriculture and Peasant Industry in Eighteenth-Century Flanders', in [74]; reprinted in [54]. Contains much of the empirical evidence on which the generalizations contained in [64] are based.

[66] F.F. Mendels, 'Seasons and Regions in Agriculture and Industry During the Process of Industrialization', in S. Pollard (ed.), *Region und Industrialisierung* (1980). Argues that cottage industry was located in regions of subsistence agriculture.

[67] D.R. Mills, 'Proto-industrialization and Social Structure: The Case of the Hosiery Industry in Leicestershire, England', in [28].

[68] R. Millward, 'The Emergence of Wage Labor in Early Modern England', *Explorations in Economic History*, 8 (1981). An ingenious if not entirely convincing analysis.

[69] H.A. Miskimin, *The Economy of Early Renaissance Europe, 1300–1460* (1969). Contains a useful survey of late-medieval developments in the European textile industry.

[70] J. Mokyr, *Industrialization in the Low Countries, 1795–1850* (1976). A theoretical and empirical study of Belgium and the Netherlands.

[71] J. Mokyr, *Why Ireland Starved: A Quantitative and Analytical History of the Irish Economy, 1800–1850* (1983). Concerned with deindustrialization only as part of a larger study of the Irish economy. Stresses shortages of capital and low labour productivity.

[72] J.U. Nef, *The Rise of the British Coal Industry*, 2 vols (1932). Stresses the importance of industrial development in the sixteenth and seventeenth centuries. Responsible for the notion of industrial progress in Britain as a series of revolutions.

[73] E. O'Malley, 'The decline of Irish Industry in the Nineteenth Century', *The Economic and Social Review*, 13 (1981). Re-

views explanations of deindustrialization and concludes that it was the result of the tendency of industries to centralize.

[74] W.N. Parker and E.L. Jones (eds), *European Peasants and their Markets* (1975). Contains eight essays on various aspects of agriculture and European economic development.

[75] F. Perlin, 'Proto-industrialization and Pre-colonial South Asia', *Past & Present*, 98 (1983). An application of the concept to non-European societies.

[76] S. Pollard, *Peaceful Conquest: The Industrialization of Europe 1760–1970* (1981). Part I is a comprehensive survey of European industrialization to the 1870s and includes a discussion of proto-industrialization.

[77] G.D. Ramsay, *The English Woollen Industry, 1500–1750* (1982). An excellent, up-to-date introduction.

[78] D.A. Reid, 'The Decline of Saint Monday, 1776–1876', *Past & Present*, 71 (1976). A review of working practices in the Birmingham metal trades.

[79] *Revue Du Nord*, LXI (1979). Special issue 'Aux origines de la révolution industrielle. Industrie rurale et fabriques'. Twelve articles on aspects of industrialization in continental Europe.

[80] W.W. Rostow, 'The Stages of Economic Growth', *Economic History Review*, 2nd ser., XII (1959). A succinct summary of [81].

[81] W.W. Rostow, *The Stages of Economic Growth* (1960). A modern version of nineteenth-century stage theories. Has greatly influenced thinking on the nature of economic development.

[82] M.B. Rowlands, *Masters and Men in the West Midland Metalware Trades before the Industrial Revolution* (1975). A detailed local study concentrating on industrial organization and social relations.

[83] W. Seccombe, 'Marxism and Demography', *New Left Review*, 137 (1983). Attempts to incorporate long-term demographic change into Marxist interpretations of capitalist development.

[84] J. Stuart, *Historical Memoirs of the City of Armagh (1819)*.

[85] P. Sweezy, 'A Critique [of Maurice Dobb]', in [40]. Part of the Marxist debate on the origins of capitalism. See [29].

[86] J. Tann, 'The Textile Millwright in the Early Industrial Revolution', *Textile History*, 5 (1974). A useful empirical study.

[87] J. Thirsk, 'Industries in the Countryside', in F.J. Fisher (ed.), *Essays in the Economic History of Tudor and Stuart England in Honour of R.H. Tawney* (1961); reprinted in J. Thirsk, *The Rural Economy of England: Collected Essays* (1984). An important statement of the association between farming regions and rural industry in England.

[88] J. Thirsk, 'The European Debate on Customs of Inheritance', in [33]; reprinted in J. Thirsk, *The Rural Economy of England: Collected Essays* (1984). A survey of contemporary thought on inheritance customs.

[89] C. Tilly and R. Tilly, 'Agenda for European Economic History in the 1970s', *Journal of Economic History*, XXXI (1971). Responsible for the first use of the word 'proto-industrialization' in print and anticipates ideas developed in [64].

[90] L.A. Tilly, 'Individual Lives and Family Strategies in the French Proletariat', *Journal of Family History*, 4 (1979). Develops the concept of 'family strategies' as a way of explaining individual behaviour during industrialization.

[91] A. Toynbee, *Lectures on the Industrial Revolution in England* (1884). Introduced the idea of the industrial revolution into English historiography a century ago and still worth reading.

[92] H. Van Der Wee, 'Structural Changes and Specialization in the Industry of the South Netherlands, 1100–1600', *Economic History Review*, 2nd ser., XXVIII (1975). An example of late-medieval adaptation in the textile industry, including the development of rural manufacturing, in response to market changes.

[93] G. Unwin, *Industrial Organization in the Sixteenth and Seventeenth Centuries* (1904). An early and still important discussion of the evolution of industrial organization. Influenced by the stage theories discussed in [45].

[94] R. Wall, J. Robin and P. Laslett (eds), *Family Forms in Historic Europe* (1983). Seventeen essays discussing the household in its economic and social context. See also [56].

[95] R.G. Wilson, 'The Supremacy of the Yorkshire Cloth Industry in the Eighteenth Century', in [36]. Stresses the importance of superior organization rather than labour costs in explaining Yorkshire's supremacy.

[96] E.A. Wrigley and R.S. Schofield, *The Population History of England 1541–1871: A Reconstruction* (1981). A masterpiece.

Chapters 10 and 11 relate long-term population and economic trends.

[97] A. Young, *Tour in Ireland: with General Observations on the General State of that Kingdom* (1780).

Index

Dent 25
Dobb, M. 12
dressmakers *see* clothing industries
dual occupations 19, 38, 53
    see also cottage industries;
            farmer-manufacturers;
            peasant-manufacturers;
            putting-out; rural industries
Dublin 25
dyeing 16

East Anglia 16, 32, 33, 34, 37
East Midlands 25
economic development 11, 12, 14,
    37, 56–7
embroidering 41, 56
emigration 47
England 11, 17, 24, 25, 26, 29, 30,
    31, 32, 34, 35, 36, 37, 42, 43,
    46, 52, 53, 54
Essex 46

factory industry 10, 12, 14, 15,
    19, 27, 28, 29, 30, 31, 32–3, 34,
    35–6, 37, 38, 51, 52, 54
    see also centralized workshops
family:
    formation 13, 39–40, 42–3,
        47–8
    labour 23, 35, 40, 47–8
    life cycle 40–1
    size 41, 47, 55–6
    structure 44, 47–8
    see also household
'family strategies' 48
farmer-manufacturers 10, 22, 23,
    47
    see also cottage industries;
        dual occupations;
        peasant-manufacturers;
        putting-out; rural
        industries
farmer-weavers *see*
        farmer-manufacturers
fertility 40, 44, 45, 46, 47
feudalism 12, 13, 22, 36–7, 40
Flanders 16, 18, 22, 26, 34, 45, 49
footwear *see* leather industries

framework-knitting 15, 22, 26,
    44–5, 46, 47, 49, 53
    see also hosiery
France 16, 34, 37, 43

Germany 16, 18
Ghent 26
gilds 19, 20
Gloucestershire 17, 20, 37
Greenwood, J. 33

Halifax 26
historical economists 12, 14
hosiery 21, 22, 35, 53
household:
    formation 10
    functions 10, 39–40
    size 10, 42–3, 48, 55–6
    structure 10, 39, 42–3, 48, 55–6
    see also family
Huddersfield 26

immiseration 10, 42, 49–50, 56
industrial development 11, 13, 51,
    52
    see also industrialization;
        industrial revolution
industrial revolution 9, 11, 12,
    13, 29,
    see also industrial development,
        industrialization
industrialization 10, 13, 54–5
    see also industrial development;
        industrial revolution
inheritance customs 39, 43, 44, 45
Ireland 17, 25, 34, 35–6, 38, 45,
    47, 53, 55
ironmongers 25
iron-smelting 15, 54
    see also metal-smelting

Jones, E.L. 13

labour:
    cost of 15, 19–20, 28, 30, 31,
        34–5, 39, 52, 53, 54, 55, 56
    demand for 28, 30, 41
    family 23, 35, 40, 55–6
    markets 14, 31

saddlery *see* leather industries
St Monday 29
Saxony 16
Schofield, R.S. 30, 46
Scotland 25
scythes *see* metal-working
    industries
Sheffield 19
Shepshed 26, 44, 45, 46, 47, 49
shoemaking *see* leather industries
Silesia 16, 22, 24, 34, 36–7
silk 16, 18, 19, 37
Skipton 25
Smith, Adam 53
Somerset 20, 37
Spain 18
spinners, spinning 18, 23, 24, 26,
    31, 35, 41, 45, 48, 52, 56
spinning jennies 31
spinning wheels 16
stocking-knitting *see*
    framework-knitting
stockings *see* hosiery
Strutt, Jedediah 32
Stuart, J. 23
Suffolk 20, 53
Sussex 34
Switzerland 13, 45–6

tailors *see* clothing industries
tanning *see* leather industries
tariffs 36, 37
Terling 46
textile industry 9, 10, 13, 16, 17,
    18, 19, 20–1, 26, 32, 35, 37, 45,
    53, 55
  see also cloth; cotton; linen; new
      draperies; silk; woollen
      industry
Thirsk, J. 13, 20, 21, 43
Tilly, C. 11
Tilly, L. 48
Tilly, R. 11
towns:
  as commercial centres 9, 16,
      25–6, 51, 53

  industry in 15, 26, 51, 53–4
Toynbee, A. 11
trade:
  international 9, 10, 13, 14, 15,
      17, 26, 34, 36, 37, 40, 41–2,
      51, 52, 54,
  local 15, 27, 51
Twente 16

Ulster 16, 17, 18, 21, 22, 23, 25,
    26, 34, 35–6, 47–8, 49, 53
underemployment 15, 20, 28, 39
Unwin, G. 14

wage-earners 12, 23, 24, 26, 41,
    50, 56
wages 30, 31, 39, 41, 49, 50
Wakefield 26
Walsall 19
Watt, J. 33
Weald, the 21, 34
weavers, weaving 15, 18, 23, 24,
    26, 35, 36–7, 41, 45, 48, 49, 52
West of England 32, 34, 37
West Midlands 19, 23–4, 29, 49
Westmorland 21
Westphalia 16
West Riding 16, 17, 21, 23, 25, 37
wheelrights 33
Wiltshire 17, 20, 25, 37, 53
woollen industry 16, 17, 18, 19,
    23, 24, 31–2, 34, 35, 37, 52,
    53–4
  see also new draperies; textile
      industry; worsteds
worsteds 21, 23, 24, 37
  see also textile industry; woollen
      industry
Wrigley, E.A. 30, 46
Wupper valley 18

Yorkshire 17, 21, 25, 32, 37, 49
Young, Arthur 21, 49

Zurich 45–6, 48